THE COMPLETE
PERSONAL
PENSIONS

by

JENNY HARRIS

Rushmere Wynne
England

First published by Rosters Ltd 1989
This edition 1996

© JENNY HARRIS

All rights reserved. No part of this publication may be reproduced, stored in a retrieval system, or transmitted, in any form or by any means, electronic, mechanical, photocopying, recording or otherwise, without the prior permission of the publishers.

The right of Jenny Harris to be identified as the author of this work has been asserted by her in accordance with the Copyright, Designs and Patents Act 1988.

British Library Cataloguing in Publication Data. A catalogue record for this book is available from the British Library.

ISBN 0 948035 30 7

Designed and typeset by:
MacWing

Published by:
Rushmere Wynne Limited
4-5 Harmill, Grovebury Road,
Leighton Buzzard, Bedfordshire LU7 8FF
Tel: 01525 853726
Fax: 01525 852037

Printed by:
H. S. Printers
4-5 Harmill, Grovebury Road,
Leighton Buzzard, Bedfordshire LU7 8FF

THE COMPLETE GUIDE TO PERSONAL PENSIONS

by

JENNY HARRIS

Rushmere Wynne
England

CONTENTS

Acknowledgements	7
Introduction	9
Chapter 1 Where to begin planning your pension	15
Chapter 2 What the state provides	41
Chapter 3 Understanding company pensions	59
Chapter 4 Personal pensions	95
Chapter 5 How to choose a personal pension	123
Chapter 6 Using PEPs to pep up your pension	147
Chapter 7 Making the best of your pension	159
Glossary of main terms	193
Index	203
Reference sources	205

ACKNOWLEDGEMENTS

The author would like to acknowledge, with very warm appreciation, the invaluable and painstaking technical support on the back doubles of pensions law given by:

Steven Meredith
Personal Financial Planning Adviser for Clerical Medical & General Life Assurance Society (which produces those beautiful advertisements on television!).

Any errors that might have crept in are entirely due to the author.

Thanks Steve!

INTRODUCTION

Pension planning can be fun. While at one end of the spectrum you may feel it is rather like picking horses at the races, at a more realistic level it's rather like planning an exciting holiday. The timescale may be different but the objective is the same – because pensions are designed to make sure you have enough income on which to retire in comfort and spend all your time 'on holiday'.

Retirement planning is all about building up a good fund over a long period to help some of your dreams come true when you retire and put away the tools of your trade, when you don't have to go to the office every day, and when you have masses of time to indulge yourself and your family.

There is one golden rule about retirement funding – the earlier you start the better off you will be in retirement. It certainly isn't something to be left until middle age, so we have especially taken into account youngsters in their twenties in an effort to encourage them to start early.

It is vital to realise that there is no such thing as a retirement funding strategy that suits everyone. Because all individuals have their own requirements, you cannot hope to get an off-the-peg design that is right for you. You need to look at the various options and, probably with professional advice, select the pattern that suits you best. We hope this book helps you to understand the ground rules and that it pushes you in the right direction.

Most retirement planning may centre on the critical element of choosing the right sort of tax-efficient pension scheme to ensure you have enough income. However, nowadays it includes the exciting *Personal Equity Plans* (PEPs) which can be used to top up your retirement income. These help you to control your finances and give retirement planning an interesting new dimension. While concentrating on the various types of pension option open to you, this book will look at the advantages of using PEPs to pep up your retirement portfolio.

Apart from being fun, planning for retirement is now becoming increasingly necessary because, with the best will in the world, state pension schemes couldn't be expected to keep up with the population's demands. As each decade passes, people's standards of living increase. At its simplest, who would have thought 20 years ago that the majority of households in the UK – some 80% of them – would have a video recorder; or that dishwashers would have become almost as indispensable as washing machines; or that holidays abroad and long weekend breaks would become so popular?

State pension schemes, for which people contributed throughout their working lives through *National Insurance contributions*, are really designed to give them a safety net. They were never intended to indulge people in their desire for the good life. But the safety net has become rather frayed. The Government is committed to reducing the individual's reliance on the state. The 'cradle to grave' philosophy has gone

INTRODUCTION

forever. Governments all over the industrialised world are making people more conscious of the need to plan for their own retirement.

While not planning to eliminate state pensions altogether, the Government argues that taxpayers simply won't be able to afford to keep paying more and more for the older people's state pension. Its value will gradually reduce to a level where it barely keeps people off the poverty line. The reason is that the population of industrialised countries is getting older, as families have fewer babies, and increasingly after the year 2000 there will be fewer people at work to support those in retirement.

At the same time, people are living longer because, generally, they are healthier. Not long ago, few people could expect to be retired for more than five to 10 years. But now many people are surviving well into their eighties and nineties. The Queen is overloaded with requests for the telegram she traditionally sends to congratulate people on their 100th birthday. This means that many people can expect to be in retirement for almost as long as they were at work – 30 to 40 years! That's a long 'holiday' and needs more careful planning than a two-week tour of the Greek islands.

Women are especially vulnerable to the problem of the 'long holiday' because they will never achieve equality with men in one important area of life: most can expect to spend more time in retirement as they tend to live longer than men. Despite this they tend to rely on their husband's pension. This is dangerous. It could leave them with very little, especially if they get divorced. One in three marriages ends in divorce – so it is a real threat.

The law is in the process of changing: divorced wives will

soon have a claim on their ex-husband's pension, but what if: a) he doesn't have one, or has a very small one; and b) by his retirement he has had a couple of wives or acquired new dependants who can claim a share as well? Even with the proposed law change, ex-wives can only claim (as opposed to get) the share of the husband's pension that was built up while they were married.

In addition, if the wife/widow remarries or co-habits with another man, her claim on her original husband's pension could be threatened. This all adds up to one sensible conclusion: women should ensure they have a pension in their own right.

On a more positive side, the UK government isn't washing its hands of pensions. While it wishes to pay out less, and certainly doesn't want to pay out more, it does offer generous tax concessions to encourage people to help themselves. Options include: joining the company pension scheme, if the company has one, and perhaps topping it up with other plans; setting up a *personal pension* plan, which is your main option if you are self-employed; and investing in *Personal Equity Plans*.

There is also scope for building up your retirement 'pot' by other savings plans and investing on the Stockmarket and in unit trusts, but they do not offer any tax advantages and are beyond the scope of this book (see Neil Stapley's book: *The Private Investor's Guide to the Stockmarket*. Details are given on page 202).

The route you take depends on your individual circumstances, such as your age and how long you have to go before retirement, your family commitments, your occupation and income, your financial prospects and, of course, what you plan to do in retirement, if you know yet.

But even if retirement is too far away to worry about how

INTRODUCTION

you are going to spend your time, what is sure is that if you don't start planning your pension and checking what you already have, you are risking a miserable and poverty-stricken retirement.

If retirement is just round the corner and you think your plans are all on course, there is no harm in conducting a personal audit of your pension position. It may not be as good as you think and you may have time to improve on it – you may even find yourself in a position to retire earlier than you thought.

How do you decide which way to turn when the choices are seemingly endless? Do not despair. In this book we take you step by step through the pensions maze and show you which key points you need to consider along the way in order to make the most of your pension planning.

We have tried to make this book as easy to read and as jargon free as possible, but some special terms are inevitable. Don't worry, many are included in a glossary at the back of the book and all are explained in the chapters which follow.

In chapter one we take a broad brush approach, looking at the many options open to you – whatever age you are. Strategies are suggested for each age band, whether you are in your twenties, thirties, forties or fifties. In subsequent chapters we will expand on the points made. **(Key terms, which will be explained in the book, are printed in *italics*.)**

Chapter 1:
Where to begin planning your pension

A sensible start to pension planning is to ask yourself three basic questions:

1 How much will you need when you retire?
2 How much will you have if you do nothing?
3 If you are not going to have enough, how can you make up the shortfall?

The answer to all these questions depends on your age. So if you are 20-something some of these questions might be rather more academic than if you are 50-something. Nevertheless, it is wise to set yourself some sort of goal – even if you move the goalposts later.

If you are 20-something you probably have no idea of how much you will need. You might fancy retiring in your fifties and playing golf or bridge three days a week, and spending the rest of the time on holiday visiting all those exotic places you never had time to see before.

If you are in your thirties, struggling to keep up with the demands of a young growing family, you will probably have a better idea of your retirement aims – be it financial security and the quiet life, or even a hectic life catching up on all those things you can't afford to do now.

By the time you are in your forties, the chances are that your children are very expensive – but the costs should peak during this decade and give you the opportunity to focus more finances on enjoying yourself without the financial restraints imposed by having children. If you work out what you want from retirement, and organise your finances well now, it should hopefully be downhill all the way towards a contented retirement.

If you are 50-something you should have a better idea of what you want from retirement, from setting up the business you always wanted to sitting down and watching all those films you never had time to enjoy before.

Whatever age you are, you need to take into account certain principles. In this chapter we first look at the fundamentals of pension planning and then at suitable strategies for the various age groups.

How much pension will you need?

It is generally accepted that most people will need a pension of two-thirds of their final salary at retirement in order to maintain their lifestyle. But it is difficult to generalise because this obviously depends on your individual circumstances. Therefore, it is sensible to begin with a personal audit of income and expenditure in order to establish how much pension you would need to maintain your present lifestyle and any adjustments you may require in future.

Although it is probably impossible to fill in such an audit completely accurately, it will give you a pretty good idea of how you would stand. Drawing up the list is rather like playing snakes and ladders, you will find you win some and you lose some, but fill them in at today's prices and don't worry about inflation for the moment:

– **OUT go** items such as your mortgage, because that will generally have been paid off by retirement; fares to work – that could be a lot if you commute from the country into your nearest city; private education; endowment policy premiums if the policies mature at retirement; National Insurance; and, of course, pension contributions!

– **DOWN go** items that will normally be reduced, including: taking the children on holiday, or paying for them to go on expensive school trips; expenses for the car (unless you have a company car).

– **UP go** items that will increase, such as car expenses, if you have used a company car for work; heating and lighting, because you will probably spend more time at home; hobbies, because you will have more time to enjoy yourself; and possibly more holidays now you have the time.

After you have made the necessary adjustments, let's assume you have come to the magic two-thirds final salary. You therefore need to check what you may be earning when you retire:

Table 1: What your present earnings will be worth if they increase by 5% a year until retirement.

Years to retirement	Salary £10,000	£20,000	£30,000	£40,000
5	12,762	25,524	38,286	51,048
10	16,288	32,573	48,864	65,155
15	20,788	41,576	62,364	83,157
20	26,531	53,062	79,593	106,124
25	33,861	67,727	101,583	135,444
30	43,216	86,432	129,648	172,864
35	55,155	110,310	165,465	220,620

From **Table 1** above you can see that if your salary is £10,000 a year now, your salary will be £16,288 in 10 years' time if you get annual increases of 5%; and that it will rise to £55,155 in 35 years' time, if it increases at the same rate. Of course, it is unlikely that your salary will rise by exactly 5% a year, but this is a rough estimate to give you some idea on what basis to do your calculation.

To work out what this means in terms of pensions provision is another matter, and later (in Chapter 7) we will go more closely into the question of pension *annuities* (incomes for life). For the moment, for illustrative purposes, let's use the nicely rounded rule-of-thumb measurement and assume that a suitable 10% *annuity* will be available. This means that for every £1,000 of gross annual income you want in retirement, you will need a pension fund of £10,000.

The important thing to bear in mind is that inflation – regardless of which political party is running the country – will inevitably erode your funds. It is better to overestimate its impact than to underestimate it.

If you are lucky, your earnings may increase faster than inflation, but they may equal inflation, in which case you will effectively be standing still. However, it is salutary at this stage to see the effect inflation could have on the purchasing power of any capital you may have.

Table 2: Examples of the declining purchasing power of £10,000 at various levels of inflation.

Inflation at	3%	5%	7.5%
	£	£	£
After 1 year	9,700	9,500	9,250
After 2 years	9,400	9,020	8,550
After 3 years	9,120	8,570	7,910
After 4 years	8,850	8,140	7,320
After 5 years	8,580	7,730	6,770
After 10 years	7,370	5,980	4,580
After 15 years	6,330	4,630	3,100
After 20 years	5,430	3,580	2,100

From this table you can see that if your income remained absolutely level at, say, £10,000 a year, and inflation stayed at the exceptionally low average of 3% a year, in 20 years' time your income will be worth only half as much as it is now, in terms of what you can buy with it. It follows, then, that the greater the level of inflation the worse the situation becomes.

How much pension have you got in the bag?

Basically, your retirement income will be based on any pensions for which you have already qualified and any capital you have been able to accumulate by then. You will need to establish how much you can expect from each source

- under the state scheme;
- from your current and previous employers;
- from any *personal pension* or self-employed pension you have built up.

State pensions

There are two main state pension schemes. These are the *basic state pension* and the *State Earnings Related Pension Scheme* (SERPS), which tops up your state pension according to your earnings. In the next chapter we explain how each works, and how your local office of the Department of Social Security (DSS) can provide you with information about your state benefits on retirement.

At the present time, under normal circumstances, a married couple can expect a basic state pension of £61.15 a week (£3,179.80 a year) on retirement, plus £36.60 a week (£1,903.20 a year) *additional pension* for married women. This totals £97.75 a week (£5,083 a year) for a married couple

If, however, both spouses qualify for a full basic state pension in their own right they will not get the married woman's pension as well. A married couple will qualify for whichever combination gives them the largest income.

If the wife, for example, has not qualified for a full basic pension but has qualified for a pension in excess of the married woman's *additional pension* of £36.60 a week (£1,903.20 a year), then she will draw that instead of the married woman's pension.

When making long-term plans you can assume that the basic pension will remain fairly constant in cash terms because historically, regardless of the political complexion of the Government of the day, it is inflation-proofed. However, while it is increased each year, it is not increased in line with average pay but with retail prices, which generally don't rise as fast. Therefore, the younger you are now, the smaller the state pension you can expect in comparison with your pay. It has already fallen to 17% of average earnings and could be down to 10% by the time you retire.

You may also be eligible for some *State Earnings Related Pension Scheme* (SERPS) pension if you have been employed by a company in any period since April 1978. However, not everyone is entitled to this because some company pension schemes opt out of SERPS (usually called *contracting-out*). And since 1 July 1988 individuals have been allowed to contract-out personally, if they buy a certain type of *personal pension* called an *Appropriate Personal Pension*.

Company pensions

If you are in a company pension scheme, the scheme administrators **should** send you a statement every year (in fact it is your legal right) telling you how much pension you have accumulated so far and how much you will receive if you stay in the scheme until normal retirement age.

If you are in a *final salary* scheme, you can make your own estimate of what you can expect, provided you have a copy of the company scheme rule book, which will explain the finer points. They do vary from company to company. In Chapter 3 we explain how to calculate this figure yourself.

Because final salary benefits are tied to the salary you are getting when you retire, your ultimate pension is reasonably predictable – it is in proportion to your pay and the number of years you have been in the company scheme. How much that will be in pounds and pence is less important if you are going to qualify for a full two-thirds final salary pension – and very few people do, though they often think they will. However, you may get into financial difficulties on retirement if you cannot put in enough time to qualify for the full (two-thirds) pension and need to top it up with another pension.

Also you may have difficulties if you are in a company's *money purchase* scheme, or have a *personal pension*. In both of these the ultimate value of your pension fund is totally linked to the performance of the fund in which your contributions are invested.

Personal pensions, money purchase schemes and AVCs

If you are in a *money purchase* company scheme, or a *personal pension* scheme, your last statement from your pension provider will tell you how much money you have built up in your fund. The *annuity* table (**Table 8** on page 76) explains how to estimate the amount of pension your fund will provide. You could also use this table to estimate how much your retirement savings could generate if necessary.

Previous employments

In post-war Britain the workforce has become very mobile, moving from job to job and few people have been lucky enough to stay in the same job for any length of time, especially in the uncertain economic climate of recent years. Therefore, many people will have had a number of jobs in their working life. If this has happened to you, it would be sensible to track down any pension rights you may have earned from past employers (if you were in their pension scheme) to establish how much you can expect from them. If you have difficulty in tracing former employers, you should contact the **Pensions Scheme Registry**, PO Box 1NN, Newcastle upon Tyne NE99 1NN, who will try to help.

If you have more than, say, 10 years to go before retirement, and you were in a *final salary* scheme, it may be sensible to consider getting these pension rights transferred to your own *personal pension*, or to a *Buy-out plan* (also called a Section 32 pension). But it is essential that you take professional advice before doing this to make sure that it is the right decision for your particular case. The company will not be able to give you the money, but may transfer it to your own fund. This will give you more control over your pension planning and could save you the heartbreak of seeing your pension rights from previous employers eroded by inflation. You can usually only do this if you were in a company pension scheme for at least two years (five years before 1988), but you might be pleasantly surprised at how much you have accumulated.

If you were in a company *money purchase* scheme, you will probably be better off leaving the money in that fund. But in any case it is worth asking the crucial question – 'How much is my fund?' – and discussing the matter with your financial adviser.

AGE by AGE

We now look at some sensible strategies for the different ages of pensions investors.

20-somethings

People in their twenties, or even their teens, are the lucky ones: they have all the benefits of recent pension changes, with the widest range of options of all time. People close to retirement are really envious of the pension opportunities open to the younger generation.

In the past the only pension schemes available were offered by companies to selected, usually senior and professional, members of staff. Even then, staff could only join if invited and after a long qualifying period of employment. Even when they allowed more people to join, many company schemes discriminated against *early leavers* – often a euphemism for people who have been made redundant – and gave them vastly reduced pensions, sometimes as little as nothing, without any inflation-proofing. But now the rules have changed. Pension schemes are far more democratic and companies with a pension scheme usually encourage full-time – and even part-time – workers to join, and they must offer minimum levels of inflation-proofing to *early leavers'* pensions as well as to those who last the distance to retirement.

The great thing about being in your twenties now is that you can call some of the shots. You can choose to join the company pension scheme if you wish, or you can go it alone with a *personal pension*.

Which route should you choose?

If you expect to stay with your employers for the whole of your working life, and if your employers have a good *final salary* scheme, preferably based on 1/60ths (see Chapter 3) then you should seriously consider joining it. This will ensure that your pension keeps pace with your earnings. If you work with them for the full 40 years, you should be assured of an inflation-proofed pension of two-thirds of your salary at retirement.

However, not many people in their twenties can be sure of staying with the same employer for that length of time. People such as career civil servants, local authority employees, teachers and National Health Service employees are more fortunate in this respect because if they change jobs within the public sector they can usually transfer their pension rights with them. It's as though they had stayed in the same job.

Employees in the private sector are more likely voluntarily to change jobs from time to time to further their careers, and are more likely to be made redundant. They are therefore more likely to benefit from a *personal pension* to which they can contribute, regardless of which company they work for or whether they become self-employed. Employers may even be prepared to contribute to it as well. If your employers are **not** prepared to contribute to a *personal pension*, it may well be that they have their own scheme – which is better because it may offer a better deal, with widow/ers' *death in service benefits* and life cover.

The younger you are when you start contributing to a major investment such as a pension, the longer time it has to build up. Initially you may not be able to afford much, but if you are financially disciplined and increase your pension contributions as you earn more, you can get your pension underpinned from an early age.

If you should later be employed by a company with a super pension scheme, you can join it and leave your personal pension on ice, and it will continue building up. You can't be in both a company pension scheme and continue contributing to your *personal pension* at the same time – unless you take advantage of the *carry-back arrangements*.

One advantage of having a *personal pension* is that, if you should later wish to retire early, you are allowed to start drawing it from age 50, whereas most company schemes base their pension on the expectation that you will work until 'normal' retirement age. This may not be the same as the state retirement age, it could be younger. People in their twenties now can expect a state retirement age of 65 whether they are male or female.

How much should you contribute?

This is a very difficult question to answer for people in their twenties. A minimum of 5% of your normal earnings would seem to be rock bottom, especially as you would be expected to pay this much into most company schemes. You should aim to increase this 5% to a higher percentage as your earnings improve. However, it would be more realistic for you (perhaps in partnership with your employer) to pay at least 15% of your earnings for every year of your working life. In round figures, even if you start at age 20, you will need to save 15% of your pay every year to buy a pension from age 60 of half of what you are earning then. Leave it to age 40, and you will need to set aside 35% each year.

A realistic level is probably the maximum that the Inland Revenue allows for people aged under 36 – that is 17.5% of your normal earnings. You can always reduce your contributions later if you think that is more than enough. The later you build up your funds the more you have to contribute to keep your fund on course.

Checklist for twenties

The following is a checklist of the action you would be advised to take to ensure that your pension plans are well in hand:

If you are in a *company pension* scheme:

- Read the scheme handbook carefully, and then check the last annual statement you received to find out the level of pension you can expect. Don't forget that your employer **must** contribute to the company scheme.

- If it is a *final salary* scheme based on **60ths,** your pension should be good if you stay, so you need not worry for the time being. But keep an open mind in case your circumstances change, such as wanting to retire early.

- If it is a *final salary* scheme based on **80ths,** it will be virtually impossible for you to clock up enough years to get a full two-thirds pension, because you would need to stay in it for 53 years! You should consult your financial adviser about making *additional voluntary contributions* (AVCs) or making alternative investments. However, if you are a civil servant or work in local government your final salary will be based on 80ths, but as you will also get a lump sum on top, the pension is equivalent to a 60ths scheme.

- If it is a *money purchase* scheme check that the combined contributions of you and your employer are at least 15%. If less, consider making *additional voluntary contributions.*

If you have a *personal pension:*

- If you are earning more than about £11,000 a year, have you *contracted-out* of SERPS, using your National Insurance rebate? If you are not contributing your SERPS rebate to your *personal pension* you could ask your pension provider, or financial adviser, for details about how to contract-out. They will make it easy for you, providing you with the necessary form to fill in which they then send to the DSS.
- If you have a SERPS *rebate-only* pension – you should consider adding regular contributions of your own. You can add anything up to 17.5% of your normal earnings.

If you are not in any *pension scheme:*

- If you are planning a career in the fast lane and are paying, or are likely to pay, higher-rate tax, one of the best investments is a *personal pension.* Based on the higher rate of tax of 40% (1996/97) you get £40 rebate for every £100 you invest, or a £24 rebate for every £100 if you are a standard-rate taxpayer.
- If you are employed but currently short of money, and a company pension scheme isn't suitable, you could consider starting a *personal pension* with your 5.37% National Insurance rebate without having to face any extra outlay. You are effectively trading in the state top-up scheme in favour of a privatised scheme which could be better value in the long term.

  However, you should not rely on a *rebate-only* pension to give you an adequate retirement income. It may be better than if you relied solely on the state, but you should make

sure that you make extra contributions as soon as you can afford to.
- If, understandably, at the moment you don't like the idea of tying up your money until you retire, you could consider other types of regular savings, such as *Personal Equity Plans,* and earmark them for your retirement. This is better than making no provision at all, and besides, if you do later start a *personal pension* you may be able to transfer some of the money into it to give it a good start.

If you are self-employed:
- You are on your own. Unless you do something, you will have to rely on the basic state pension. You should be aware that you will not qualify for a SERPS pension, the state top-up scheme, apart from any SERPS you may have qualified for through previous employment. Your best route is through a *personal pension*. By buying one you can save tax. For every £100 you contribute to a *personal pension*, you can knock £24 off your annual tax bill (£40 if you are paying higher-rate tax at 40%). This is provided that your pension contribution does not exceed 17.5% of your taxable earnings (earnings after expenses).

30-somethings

If you are in your thirties, it is fairly likely that you will be married, or have a partner, and that you will have children and a mortgage. Pension planning might be last on your list of priorities as you struggle to make ends meet. However, you are probably developing a lifestyle you would be reluctant to give up, so it is worth pausing to run the ruler over your pension plans to ensure that you will be able to keep up, or improve, your lifestyle in future. If you delay, you will find that higher contributions will be necessary later to generate the level of pension you require. Delay could cost you dearly.

Checklist for thirties

If you are in a company pension scheme:

- Read the company pension scheme handbook carefully. Compare it against the last annual statement you received to find out what you could expect if you remain with them.

- If you are in a *final salary* scheme based on 60ths, check whether you can put in a full 40 years' service with them. If you can, you should be on course for a good pension and need not worry for the time being. You should also check on how much of your salary is pensioned. For example, does the scheme ignore bonuses and commission and does the figure the scheme quotes include your basic state pension?

- If you are in a *final salary* scheme and cannot put in a full 40 years – for example you are 35 now and only recently joined you are likely to be looking at a pension equal to half your current pay. If you don't think that will be enough you should consider the virtues of topping up the pension with *additional voluntary contributions* (AVCs) now, rather than leaving it to later.

If you are in a final salary scheme based on 80ths (rather than 80ths plus a lump sum), then the maximum pension you could expect if you stay in the scheme from age 18 to 65 would be just over half your final pay. If you are aged 35 now, and have just joined, the maximum you could qualify for is about 37% of final salary, that is 30/80ths. This means

WHERE TO BEGIN PLANNING YOUR PENSION

a two-thirds pension you ought to consider contributing to AVCs straightaway. It will be less painful now than in a few years' time.

- If you are in a *money purchase* company pension scheme, check how much your fund is currently worth. As a rough indicator, if it is in the order of one-quarter of what you think you will need (see **Table 1,** page 18) then you need not worry now.

- If you only recently joined the company's *money purchase* scheme, you should consider making contributions to an *additional voluntary contribution* plan (AVC). The maximum you can contribute personally is 15% of your normal salary, regardless of age. There is, theoretically, no limit to how much your employer can contribute. If that will still not be enough to give you a decent pension, then you could seriously consider alternative investments such as *Personal Equity Plans* (see Chapter 6).

If you have a *personal pension:*

- If you are under 36, are you contributing your maximum 17.5% of normal earnings into your *personal pension?* And if you are aged 36 or more, are you contributing the maximum 20%?

- If your current earnings are high, you could consider contributing extra to your *personal pension* by taking advantage of previous years' unused tax relief. Anything you were entitled to contribute over the last six years, but didn't, you can pay today, and claim tax relief in the current tax year. This will give a tremendous boost to your pension fund and may enable you to choose between retiring early, having a better pension or not having to worry about pension contributions later on.

If you are not in a pension scheme at all:

- You should seriously think about the financial implications of living on a basic state pension, currently £3,179.80 a year (1996/97), plus any other savings you have. Time is beginning to run out before pension planning gets really expensive. But you could contract out of SERPS and pay the money into your special *personal pension*. Over-thirties get a 1% incentive from the DSS, and are allowed a potential rebate of 6.37% of all earnings between £61 a week and £455.

40-somethings

As far as pension planning is concerned, the forties are a crucial period. You still have time to top up without too much pain. By now you should be less worried about the financial commitments of bringing up a family and have the time to concentrate on your own long-term future. If you want to retire on anything like two-thirds final salary your pension plans should be well under control. If they are not, then you need to consider ways of making up the shortfall.

It is estimated that, if you have done nothing so far about pension planning, you will need to set aside 35% each year (perhaps in partnership with your employer) to buy a pension from age 60 of half of what you are earning at 40 – bearing in mind inflation.

Checklist for forties

If you are in a *company pension* scheme:

- And it is a *final salary* scheme based on 60ths, and you expect to be able to have put in 40 years before you retire, then you have nothing to worry about, because you should get two-thirds final salary without any problem.

- If you cannot complete 40 years, or if you are in a scheme based on 80ths, you cannot achieve two-thirds without topping up your pension plans with *additional voluntary contributions* (AVCs) or perhaps investing in *Personal Equity Plans*.

  Alternatively, it may be possible for you to increase your pensions contributions to buy *'added years'*. Not all company schemes allow this but, if yours does, it is a convenient way of increasing your pension. Check with your scheme manager.

- Directors, executives or key workers may be able to put their pensions in the fast lane. If your firm will agree to put you on to an accelerated rate of pension, then you may be able to make up for lost time. In this way, you could be qualifying for your pension at the rate of, say, 2/60ths a year. This means that for every year you work for the firm, you get a pension of 2/60ths of a year's pay. (See Chapter 3.)

- If it is a *money purchase* scheme and your fund does not seem to match your expected requirements, then you ought to consider increasing your own contributions. The legal limit is 15% of your normal earnings but, theoretically, there is no limit to the amount the company can contribute.

If the company doesn't want to contribute, as such, it might be worth your considering a salary sacrifice arrangement. If your company agrees, you take a smaller salary and the company uses the sum you 'sacrifice' to increase its contribution to your pension fund. Your employer will save up to 10.2% in *National Insurance contributions*, therefore your contribution could be 10.2% bigger. Effectively this allows you to pay more into the scheme than the 15% of normal pay you are entitled to because your employer is paying the extra, not you. The disadvantage to you could be that any 'death in service' benefits you may be entitled to, such as four years' pay as a lump sum to your dependants if you die before getting your pension, will be reduced pro rata.

If you are contributing the maximum the *money purchase* scheme rules or the law will allow, and you will still have a shortfall, you could consider alternative investments, such as *additional voluntary contributions* (AVCs) or *Personal Equity Plans*.

If you have a *personal pension*:

- You can contribute 20% of your normal earnings, up to age 45, and then 25% up to age 50, into a *personal pension*. Therefore, if the fund seems as though it is unlikely to meet your needs, it might be a good idea to increase your contributions to this level. Alternatively, or additionally, you could consider investing in *Personal Equity Plans*.

- If you are employed and have used your *personal pension* to contract-out of SERPS, or if you are in a company money purchase scheme that is contracted-out, this is the decade that you should seriously consider contracting back in again. This will reduce your contributions to your personal pension, or your employer's *money purchase* scheme, but it is widely accepted that the benefits for contracting-in outweigh those for being contracted-out.

The Department of Social Security itself says that under the present system (1996) people who have less than 15 to 20 years left before they retire may be better off in SERPS. This is partly because National Insurance rebates invested in your funds later in life have less time to build up and earn investment returns, and partly because SERPS builds up at a higher rate for older people to reflect the fact that they will have a shorter period in SERPS. You should discuss this option with your financial adviser, or ask your pensions provider to arrange to contract-in. They are familiar with this routine – indeed in a perfect world they should write to you to advise you to do this.

If you are self-employed:

- If you already have a *personal pension*, or a *retirement annuity plan* (special policies for the self-employed which were dropped on 1 July 1988), you should review its performance and, if necessary, boost your contributions.

  For *personal pensions* the contribution limit is 20% of normal earnings to age 45, and then this increases to 25% to age 50. But, for *Retirement Annuity Plans* the limit is pegged at 17.5% until age 51 when it increases to 20%. Therefore, if you wish to increase your contributions to a level above 17.5%, you will need to start up a *personal pension*. You can run this side by side with the *Retirement Annuity Plan*, or divert all new money to the *personal pension*. It is worth asking your financial adviser which is best for you.

- You may hope to sell your business and retire on the proceeds, but this is not something you can rely on. It could be worth starting up a *personal pension* as a safety cushion, or start building up a portfolio of *Personal Equity Plans*.

If you choose the *personal pension* route, you could give it a kick-start by contributing extra to make up for some of the years you have missed. You can get tax relief on contributions made this year, using your allowance going back the previous six years.

50-somethings

People in their fifties are more likely to have been thrifty throughout their working lives because they were brought up during the era of post-war austerity. While many were denied opportunities to join pension schemes when they were young, they are more likely to have a nest-egg underpinning their retirement planning. Also an estimated 10% will have had the added *bonus* of inheriting property from their parents. People in their fifties can still give their pensions a boost. And there are some interesting options. A pension audit is critical, as you have fewer working years in which to make any adjustments.

Checklist for fifties

If you are in a *company pension* scheme:

- If you have been fortunate enough to be in a good *final salary* company pension scheme for most of your life, then you could be well on course for a really independent retirement. In this case you might be more concerned about enjoying your money and getting the best out of other investments such as *Personal Equity Plans* and TESSAs.

- If you have not been in a company *final salary* scheme for long enough, you will need to think about topping up your pension. One choice is *additional voluntary contributions* (AVCs), if you are not already contributing the full 15% of your normal earnings into your company pension.

- Another course of action, if you are a late starter in the company's final salary scheme, and are a director, an executive or key worker in the firm's *final salary* scheme, is to try to negotiate a better deal. You could ask the company to arrange your pension so that, instead of qualifying for a pension equal to 1/60th (or 1/80th) of final salary per year of service, the company counts each new year as two years.

  Therefore, if you are 50 now (in a 1/60th scheme) and expect to retire at 65, on top of what you have already qualified for, you can qualify for a half-pension in those 15 years. It follows that, if you are 55, you can get a pension worth one-third of final salary in the same time.

- If you are in a *money purchase* scheme which is not building up fast enough, you could ask the firm to let you increase your contributions up to the 15% limit of your normal earnings, if the scheme allows you to. The company may be prepared to offer you the facility of salary sacrifice, in which they drop your pay by an agreed sum and add it to your pension fund, together with your employer's National Insurance savings. Or you could look at alternative investments.

If your *money purchase* fund is really lagging behind your requirements, you could consider withdrawing from the company scheme. This means you leave your contributions invested in the company scheme and start up a *personal pension* where the contribution limits are higher. This would only be sensible if your employer is willing to contribute. Alternatively, ask whether you can pay extra into the company scheme, and then consider topping up even further, with *Personal Equity Plans*.

If you have a personal pension

- You might find the fund needs a boost and may be able to increase your contributions: at 50 you can contribute 25% of normal earnings, at 51-55 you can contribute 30%, and between 56 and 60 you can contribute 35%. This facility is ideal for late starters and those who need to give their retirement planning a tonic.
- If you have had a number of previous jobs, leaving some pension rights behind, it could be a good time to round them all up and add them to a *personal pension* or buy-out plan. You **must** take advice whether this option is right for you, but it is certainly worth investigating.

If you have no pension plan at all

- Unless you have private resources to subsidise the basic state pension, and whatever SERPS you may be entitled to, then you will need to act quickly.
- It is certainly not too late, but you have not left yourself much time. If you start a *personal pension,* then from age 46

to 50 you can contribute 25% of normal earnings (age 51-55, 30%; age 56-60, 35%; and from 61 to 74, 40%). You can always take advantage of the carry-forward facility, under which you can catch up on pension contributions for the past six years, and get the tax relief this year.

- If you have been really prudent and taken all the necessary action, absorbed all your allowances, and still wish to top up your retirement fund, you could look at alternative investments such as *Personal Equity Plans*.

The next three chapters look at state pensions, and then company pensions and on to *personal pensions*.

Chapter 2:
What the state provides

For the whole of your working life you have probably been paying *National Insurance contributions*, and perhaps wondering whether it was all worth it and what you could expect when you retire. However, when you reach the statutory pension age, which is currently 65 for men and 60 for women, you will start getting the benefit.

Historically, the official state retirement age at which people could draw their state pension was women at 60 and men at 65, but the Government has recently changed this. Under the 1995 Pensions Act, the state pension age for women is to be raised gradually from 60 to 65 between 2010 and 2020. Women who reach 60 before 2010 (that is women born before 6 April 1950) will not be affected by the changes, and will be able to draw their state pension at 60, as normal. But women born after 5 March 1955 will have to wait until they are 65 to draw their state pension. The table overleaf illustrates the retirement ages for women born between these dates.

Table 3: State pension age for women.

Some examples

Date of birth		Can draw state pension at age	
to 6 Apr	1950	60 years	
6 Apr – 5 May	1950	60 years	1 month
6 Oct – 5 Nov	1950	60 years	7 months
6 Apr – 5 May	1951	61 years	1 month
6 Oct – 5 Nov	1952	62 years	7 months
6 Apr – 5 May	1953	63 years	1 month
6 Oct – 5 Nov	1953	63 years	7 months
6 Apr – 5 May	1954	64 years	1 month
6 Oct – 5 Nov	1954	64 years	7 months
after 5 Mar	1955	65 years	

At state retirement age you stop paying *National Insurance contributions* and can at last start getting your money back through the state pension scheme, provided that you have made sufficient contributions.

The state actually provides three types of pension and when planning your retirement finances it is important to understand what you can expect from each of them. The two main pensions are:

– Basic state pension

– Additional state pension, called the *State Earnings Related Pension Scheme*, or SERPS for short.

On top of that, people who were employed between 1961 and 1975 may qualify for a Graduated Pension, which was replaced by SERPS, but at its best this is now worth only about £6 a week (£6.83 for men and £5.72 for women).

Basic state pension

The full basic state pension is paid to people who have made enough *National Insurance contributions* during their working lives. It is not enough to live on unless you are prepared to live exceedingly economically. Currently (1996/97) this is £61.15 a week (£3,179.80 a year), or £97.75 a week (£5,083 a year) for a married couple if the wife has not made sufficient contributions to earn a full basic pension in her own right.

The basic pension is reviewed and increased every year to keep pace with price inflation – which is less than earnings inflation. But while at the moment it represents something like 17% of the national average earnings for a single person, it is estimated that by 2030 the basic pension will drop to only 8.5% of national average earnings.

To qualify for the full basic pension you have to pay weekly *National Insurance contributions* for most of your working life. If you are employed, your employer deducts your payments from your earnings, adds the employer's contribution, and pays it to the Department of Social Security. If you are self-employed, you have to pay a flat-rate Class 2 contribution, usually by direct debit, once your earnings exceed £3,430 a year.

Currently (1996/97) there are four classes of National Insurance:

Class 1

Paid by all employees earning more than £60.99 a week and their employers, though some married women who opted to pay a **reduced** rate before 11 May 1977 can continue to do so. The amount the employees pay varies according to their earnings – up to a maximum of £455 a week, above which employees currently pay no more.

Class 2
Paid by all self-employed people earning more than £3,430 a year, at a flat rate of £6.05 a week.

Class 3
Voluntary contributions, currently £5.95 a week, which you can choose to pay to protect your National Insurance record if you have missed some years.

Class 4
An additional 6% levy paid by self-employed people, on top on their flat-rate contributions, on annual profits between £6,860 and £23,660. The Inland Revenue collects the money with the self-employeds' tax payment.

Basic state pension – the ground rules

To get a **full** basic state pension you must have qualifying years for about 90% of the years in your working life. A 'working life' is currently defined by the Government as 44 years for women and 49 years for men. This means that women need to have paid the full NI contributions for about 39 years and men for about 44 years. Under normal circumstances, if you have failed to pay full contributions for at least 10 years of your working life, you are not entitled to **any** basic state pension.

There are exceptions to this 10-year rule for special cases

such as anyone who takes a career break to bring up children, those who have looked after sick people, those unlucky enough to have been out of work through redundancy, illness or disability and those who were working before 1948 when the state pension scheme was introduced.

To qualify for the **minimum** basic pension payable, which is 25% of the normal pension, you normally need 10 qualifying years, which usually means that you have had to pay NI contributions for those years. However, not everyone has to pay National Insurance. You only pay it if you earn above a certain sum – currently £61 a week. If you have not earned enough to pay contributions for the whole of your working life, perhaps because you have been working part-time, your pension will normally be reduced.

In the current tax year (1996/97), anyone under state pensionable age earning £61 a week or more has to pay National Insurance at the rate of 2% on the first £61 and then 10% on all earnings between £61 and £455. This qualifies them for the basic state pension.

Married women's stamp

Earnings of married women and widows who opted to pay the reduced rate, the so-called 'married women's stamp', do not qualify towards the total of years contribution. (This option was withdrawn for newcomers in May 1977.) Wives or widows who have never paid *National Insurance contributions* cannot qualify for a state pension in their own right. However, if their husband qualifies for a state pension, then the wife qualifies for a married woman's *additional pension* based on the level of his contributions.

This *additional pension* is not available to the wife/widow until she reaches 60 and the husband reaches 65 (or would have done). However, if the husband reaches 65 – and receives his pension – before the wife reaches 60, he **may** be able to get an increase of his basic pension for his wife.

If the wife/widow qualifies for a part pension which is not equal to the full married person's 'additional' pension, she will only get the lesser pension until her husband reaches 65 and starts drawing his state pension, when her pension will be topped up to the full *additional pension* level.

At current rates (1996/97), the *additional pension* is up to £36.60 a week (£1,903.20 a year), bringing the total for the couple to £97.75 a week (£5,083 a year). However, on the death of the husband, the wife should normally receive a widow's pension of £61.15 a week (£3,179.80 a year), which is the same as a basic pension.

Career breaks

Special arrangements were introduced in April 1978 for people who stop working for a few years to bring up their children, provided they are getting child benefit for children under 16. Similar concessions apply to those people who have given up their jobs to look after a sick person and who qualify for income support. Few people seem to know this, but their basic state pension rights are protected under the Home Responsibility Protection scheme (HRP). For every year they are out of work for these reasons they should be automatically credited with one qualifying year for their pension, provided they let the DSS know. However, there is evidence that the DSS sometimes overlook this. To claim, you need to fill in form CF411 from the Benefits Agency.

Married women and widows who kept up their option to pay the reduced stamp cannot get credits under this scheme.

If you have to stop work to look after someone who is getting an attendance allowance, you should apply for HRP for those years. You must apply annually, using Form CF411 which is available from your local Department of Social Security office. Other people who can arrange to protect their pensions include those who have been receiving unemployment benefit, sickness benefits, invalidity benefit or approved training.

Divorced women

A divorced woman can use her ex-husband's insurance to protect her pension credits for the period they were married. Therefore, a woman who either did not pay *National Insurance contributions*, perhaps because she did not work or earn enough to pay, or who elected to pay the married women's stamp, need not lose out for that period, provided her husband paid the full contributions. If his contribution record is insufficient for full credits, then her credits will be scaled down accordingly. If the ex-husband remarries, his new wife will still (subject to his contribution record) qualify for the usual married woman's pension and widow's pension. The husband is treated as though he had only been married once.

The self-employed

The self-employed qualify for the basic state pension through their Class 2 flat-rate contribution. If they also have to pay Class 4 *National Insurance contributions* based on their profits, this will make no difference to their pension. A self-employed year is treated the same as an employed year. So, if you have worked for an employer in the past, those years are added to your self-employed years, provided you have kept up your regular contributions.

SERPS

SERPS (State Earnings Related Pension Scheme) is, as its name implies, the state's additional earnings-related pension scheme, but it is limited to employees. On retirement, at state retirement age, it is paid on top of the basic state pension out of the earnings-related part of *National Insurance contributions*.

It is possible for both company pension schemes and individuals to contract-out of SERPS but, if this has happened to you, you will not qualify for the state top-up scheme for the period that you are contracted-out. Some company pension schemes have opted out of SERPS in favour of getting a National Insurance rebate which they invest in their pension fund for employees, and the employees have no option. However, if it is a final salary scheme the company has to guarantee that you will not lose by the deal (see Chapter 4 for further details).

The benefits of SERPS are based solely on your earnings between the so-called *Lower Earnings Level* of £60.99 a week, as from 6 April 1996, and the Upper Earnings Level of £455 a week. The maximum anyone who retires this year (1996/97) and who has been in SERPS since it started, and who has paid the top level of contributions during that period, can expect is about £4,600.

Since the Government is committed to reducing SERPS payments, the value of this earnings-related portion will decline as from 6 April 2000. But people who are already getting a SERPS pension by then will not be affected.

Spouses

If a widow inherits a SERPS pension from her late husband, she will be paid the same sum he would have received, provided that he reaches the state retirement age of 65 before 5 April 2000. If he dies after that she will only get 50%. A widower can only inherit his late wife's SERPS pension if she had reached state retirement age before dying and if he had retired from regular employment. It can then be used to top up his own pension to the maximum SERPS any individual could qualify for. That means that if he was already getting the maximum SERPS pension he would not get any more.

The self-employed do not qualify for SERPS, but they do retain any credits they may have qualified for if they worked for an employer at some time during their working life after 6 April 1978 when SERPS was introduced. (For fuller details about SERPS, see Chapter 4: Personal pensions.)

Graduated pensions

Before SERPS was introduced there was a state pension scheme called Graduated Retirement Benefit which also related to earnings. It ran from April 1961 to April 1975 and was far from generous. However, people who have paid into it through their old *National Insurance contributions* can expect to get something from it – inflation-proofed. The maximum you can expect is about £6.82 for men and £5.71 for women – if you were well paid during that period.

Getting a state pension forecast

You can find out at any time, whatever your age, the amount of state pensions you are likely to get and what, if anything, you can do about improving them. All you have to do is get Form BR19, 'How you can get a Retirement Pension Forecast', from your local office of the Department of Social Security (their address will be in the local telephone book). You fill it in and send it back to their office in Newcastle upon Tyne, and about a month later you should get the answer. There is also Form RD171 which helps you to check your NIC record and advises what you can do if you think it is wrong. It is also useful if you want to claim Home Responsibility Protection. You can get details from the Contributions Agency, Contributions Query Section, Longbenton, Newcastle upon Tyne NE98 1YX.

The pensions forecast is a most useful asset for pension planning and it has some well-thought-out questions that you can ask, beginning 'what if. . .?' Basically the forecast will tell you:

- How much pension you are already entitled to (basic state pension, SERPS and Graduated Pension) based on your contributions so far.

- How much you will be entitled to at normal retirement age if you pay *National Insurance contributions* until then.

- What, if anything, you can do to get a better state pension.

- If you are widowed or divorced, the amount of pension you can expect from the state schemes based on your former spouse's *National Insurance contributions*.

The forecast will also tell you what may happen to your state pensions in different situations. For example, you can ask how much your pension will be if:

WHAT THE STATE PROVIDES

- You intend to carry on working past normal retirement age. You will need to give them a possible date.
- You want to retire early. You will need to give them a possible date. You won't be able to claim your pension early and it will probably be reduced.
- You want to go abroad.
- You want to start paying full-rate *National Insurance contributions* after having paid a reduced rate.
- You want to pay *National Insurance contributions* that have not been paid in the past.
- Change of marital status. You will need to give them a possible date for getting married or divorced.
- Change in annual earnings. If you expect a significant rise and are not in a *contracted-out* pension scheme this might affect your SERPS pension. Alternatively you might be expecting a drop in earnings

So, as you can see, the Department of Social Security has tried to be realistic in its approach to helping you to plan your retirement income.

When can you draw your state pensions?

The state pensions are payable when you reach the current state retirement age, whether you have retired from work or not. This retirement age is 65 for men and, as from 2010 to 2020, will gradually increase from 60 to 65 for women.

If a woman's own pension equals or exceeds the standard rate of the married woman's *additional pension*, currently £36.60

a week (£1,903.20 a year), then she will not be entitled to draw the *additional pension* as well. But if her own pension rights are less than the value of the *additional pension* then, on the retirement of her husband, she can draw a sum that brings her reduced pension up to the level of the *additional pension*.

Early retirement

People retire early for all sorts of reasons ranging from ill health to superb health (and a desire to spend their time doing their own thing rather than catching the 6.56am train to the office in the City every day), to a change of job. But retiring early requires careful planning.

The first thing to bear in mind is that if you do choose to retire early you cannot claim your *state pensions* at that stage, you will have to wait until you reach the state retirement age. But, even if you are not earning any money, you may well need to make Class 3 contributions to protect your basic state pension if you have not got enough years' credits – 39 for women and 44 for men. These contributions are made on a voluntary basis and at a flat rate – currently (1996/97) £5.95 a week.

If you are in a *company pension* scheme you may be able to draw a pension earlier than the state pension rules allow. Company pension schemes usually specify a 'normal' pension age, typically 60 or 65, but some schemes allow you to draw a company pension on early retirement at any age from 50 upwards. However, like most of the good things in life, it will be at a cost.

Final salary schemes are based on the number of years you have been in the scheme and your pay at the time you retire. Obviously if you retire early, the number of years you have put in will be reduced. Also, your pay will almost certainly be lower than it would have been if you had stayed on. On top of that, as your pension will be paid for a longer period it will cost more. However, some enlightened schemes have a policy of not applying the reduction in full, to make early retirement more attractive, especially if the company is offering voluntary redundancy.

If you are in a final salary scheme, and wish to retire early because of ill health, the company may be able to top up your pension in any case, or you may be entitled to state benefits. So you should first check with the DSS Benefits Agency office to see what you may qualify for.

Late retirement

If you are employed and wish to retire after the statutory retirement age, you don't have to pay any more *National Insurance contributions* (although your employer has to continue paying his contributions in the usual way). If you are self-employed you do not have to pay any more Class 2 contributions either, but you have to pay Class 4 contributions, based on your profits – for one more year only.

In either case, you can choose whether to draw your state pensions immediately you qualify for them or to delay drawing them until such time as you wish. By delaying drawing your state pensions you can increase their subsequent value.

Your top-up options

Currently, you can increase your state pensions by delaying drawing them for anything up to five years beyond the state retirement age. Until 5 April 2010 your pensions will increase by about 7.5% each year, and this will be inflation-proofed. From 6 April 2010 your state pensions will be increased by 10.4% a year and you can delay claiming them for as long as you want. This is to encourage people not to draw state pensions, and to save the Government some money.

Until 2010, delaying drawing your state pensions means that at the end of five years your pensions will have grown by about 37.5% over and above the rate of inflation. The decision you make on when to retire will affect all your state pensions. You cannot draw one and delay the rest.

Table 4: Effect of delaying drawing state pensions.

Example (Retiring pre-April 2010)

	Weekly this year £	Increments earned after 1 year £	after 5 years £
Basic pension	61.15	4.58	22.93
SERPS (estimate)	46.15	3.46	17.30
Graduated pension (estimate)	6.82	0.51	2.55
Total	114.12	8.55	42.78

Therefore, after one year the pensions increase from £114.12 to £122.67 and after five years they increase to £156.90 at today's figures, but it will be inflation-proofed. You will need to consider whether this is worthwhile.

If you defer your pension for five years, how long does it take to make up what you have given up? It works out that you start getting your money back in 13.3 years. The calculation below shows how to work this out, assuming current prices throughout because the inflation-proofing element will maintain the buying power of your pension:

a) Basic pension given up this year	£ 3,179.80
b) multiply by 5 (years)	x 5
c) Total pension given up	£15,899.00

To find your pension from year 6

d) pension now	£3,179.80
e) add d) x 37.5%	£1,192.42
f) enhanced pension	£4,372.22

To establish the number of years you need to draw the enhanced pension to break even:

g) divide c) by e) $\dfrac{£15,899.00}{£1,192.42}$ = 13.33 years

Therefore, a man would have to live until he was 83 before breaking even, and a woman, allowed to draw her state pension at 60, would have to live to 78. Therefore, if you are not in good health, you might be better off drawing the pensions.

Some grim-sounding so-called 'mortality' statistics might help here. A man who retires at 65 lives on average for about another 16 years, and a woman who retires at 65 lives on average for another 20 years, compared with a woman who retires at 60, who lives for another 25 years. However, if you have already started drawing your state pensions, you can arrange to stop drawing them in order to take advantage of the increments and you can start drawing them again at any time.

Any woman who is entitled to receive the married woman's *additional pension* can delay drawing it until she is 65 and still earn the 7.5% a year increases, even though her husband has started drawing his *basic state pension*. However, if a husband wants to delay drawing his state pension to earn the extra increments, and the wife is entitled to the *additional pension* from his *National Insurance contributions*, he may not do so unless the wife consents.

You will not have to pay NI contributions if you give up your pension, but if you are self-employed you may have to pay Class 4 contributions in the year of assessment in which you reach age 60 (women) or 65 (men). If you are working for an employer the employer must still pay **his** share of the contributions in the normal way. You should give your employer a Certificate of Age Exemption, form CF384, showing that you are not liable to pay contributions. You can get your state pension back whenever you want it.

The form and full details are contained in leaflet NI92, 'Giving up your Retirement Pension to Earn Extra', available from your local DSS office.

Missing years

Some people cannot hope to qualify for a full basic state pension, so they are allowed to buy in any missing years at a reduced rate while keeping up their normal payments at full rate if they are still working. These voluntary contributions are paid (1996/97) at £5.95 a week. Full details are available in leaflets CA08, 'National Insurance: Voluntary Contributions', and CA07, 'National Insurance Unpaid and Late Paid Contributions'. Both leaflets are available free from your local DSS office.

Married women and widows who opted to pay the married women's stamp are not allowed to buy back those years. However, it may be worthwhile for them to start paying the full contributions in future provided their earnings are sufficient, ie. at least £61 a week (1996/97). They may then be able to start earning credits to get a pension in their own right. But is it worth it?

It depends on your individual circumstances. In order to qualify for the minimum amount of state pension you need to clock up the equivalent of 10 years' worth of contributions at the full rate, including those years before you took up the married women's stamp option. Those 10 years will give you a quarter-pension, currently £794.95 a year. To break even, you will need to pay the full stamp for a total of 24 years. It hardly seems worth it. If you are in this position you are advised to get individual advice from your local DSS office.

More top-ups

If you have a dependent child or children for whom you are claiming child benefit when you start drawing a state pension, then you may be able to claim extra payments for each child.

Also, the Government provides a safety net for pensioners who really can't live on the state pensions. Provided that they have only minimal savings, pensioners can apply for income support to increase their income, and for housing benefit if they need help to pay the rent and/or council tax.

Conclusion

Even with all these top-ups, it is clear that few people would be able to exist satisfactorily on state pensions. So it is essential that you take charge of your own pension arrangements and try to secure a more prosperous future.

Read on. . .

Chapter 3:
Understanding company pensions

The state has made it clear that it can't afford to pay everyone a good pension, but it encourages employers to set up pension schemes for their employees. It does this by offering tax incentives to make pension provision more attractive – and some very good pension schemes have been devised. These schemes are based on the 'deferred pay' principle, so that any contributions you and your employer make are effectively part of your pay, which is invested on your behalf.

Company pension schemes (also called occupational pension schemes) are particularly good if you expect to stay with the company for any length of time, and are probably unbeatable if you will be there for the greater part of your working life. But they won't be such good value if you expect to be on the move after a couple of years, because you won't have enough time to build up your pension rights. You will lose significant amounts of pension if you leave the scheme after a short space of time, though this is gradually improving.

If you do expect to change employers several times in your working life, you should seriously consider taking out a *personal pension* instead of joining the company pension scheme. Sometimes companies which have their own pension scheme will agree to contribute to your *personal pension*. It is always worth asking when you join them.

If you are a civil servant or work for local authorities or employers like the National Health Service, you don't usually need to worry about the effect on your pension of changing jobs, provided you remain in the public sector. They run very good and flexible pension schemes and they can usually transfer your pension rights as you move on, so you shouldn't be penalised.

Also, if you are a woman, any career breaks you have, to bring up the family for instance, are less likely to interfere too much with your pension rights. You will get a smaller pension than you would if you had had an uninterrupted career, but you will usually be better off than most women in the private sector.

There are two main types of company pension scheme, and we will describe the main features of each approach and explain the pros and cons. This is designed to help you decide which is best for you, taking into account your age, likely career profile and investment attitude.

The two main types of company pension scheme are:

- *Final salary*

- *Money purchase*

There are also hybrid schemes which are a mixture of both.

Final salary

Without a doubt, a good *final salary scheme* is the Rolls-Royce of pensions, provided you have been a member for long enough to reap the benefits. This type of scheme is favoured by the Civil Service (who know what's good for them), many top international companies and, incidentally, many pension companies for their own staff.

There are currently more people in *final salary schemes* than any other type of company pension scheme. They are also known as 'defined benefit' schemes, so called because, all things being equal, you have a pretty good idea of what your pension will be: it is broadly defined when you join.

The range of benefits varies from scheme to scheme. Typically, however, you will contribute some 5% of your pay into the scheme while your employer will contribute something like 10%. Some firms have non-contributory schemes into which only the employer contributes. Either way, the money is invested in a pension fund and, regardless of how well the investment managers perform, you are guaranteed a certain level of pension – unless the firm itself collapses or decides to terminate the scheme.

The pension you get from *final salary schemes* is related directly to the amount of your salary when you retire. How much your pension will be depends on three main factors:

- your salary when you retire (or leave the scheme);
- the number of years you are in the scheme; and
- the arithmetical formula on which the scheme is based, typically 80ths or 60ths, or even (very rarely) 45ths.

If the scheme calculates pensions in 80ths, then for every year you are in the scheme you will get a pension of 1/80th of the amount of your salary at your normal retirement age. Therefore, at its simplest, if your salary at retirement is £20,000, you have been in the scheme for 20 years, and the scheme is based on 80ths, your pension will be £5,000 per annum.

It is worked out like this:

£20,000 x 20/80ths = £5,000

It is as simple as that!

If you are in an 80ths scheme and you want to achieve a company pension equal to two-thirds of your final salary, then you will need to stay with the firm for about 53 years! But if you are in a scheme based on 60ths, you will need to be a member of the scheme for a mere 40 years. In these days of high job mobility and endemic redundancy, few people are likely to stay long enough to qualify for a full two-thirds final salary. Hence there is a need to look at alternative ways to top up (see Chapter 6).

Some companies offer directors and key personnel an 'uplifting' facility, which gives them more than the standard 60ths or 80ths pension for each year that they are members of the scheme. They may, for example, give them 2/60ths, or 2/80ths, for each year they are in the scheme. If employees get 2/60ths for each year then they can qualify for a full two-thirds pension after 20 years. Likewise, if they are allowed 2/80ths they can qualify for a full two-thirds final salary pension after 27 years.

It is not possible now to qualify for a two-thirds pension in less than 20 years, but anyone who was in the pension scheme prior to 17 March 1987 may qualify for this maximum after 10 years, subject to the pension scheme rules.

Earnings cap

There is another restriction related to the maximum pension anyone can draw from an occupational scheme if they joined after 1 June 1989 (or 14 March 1989 if it was a newly founded scheme). There is now an *earnings cap*, which means that you cannot get a pension based on earnings in excess of £82,200 (1996/97). Taken together with the two-thirds rule, this means that the maximum company pension is £54,800 for 1996/97. The figures are adjusted each year, more or less in line with price inflation, the Retail Price Index. Employees who were in the scheme before the new rules applied are only limited by the two-thirds rule.

Definition

To complicate matters more, the definition of *final salary* varies from scheme to scheme. In some schemes it is literally basic salary on retirement, others include bonuses and overtime, and some are based on average salaries in the years prior to retirement. Further, some schemes add in the basic state pension when quoting you a two-thirds final salary pension! This means that they are offering to top up your basic state pension to ensure that your total pension income equals two-thirds of your final salary pension. Also, if the scheme has been contracted out of SERPS, part of the pension they quote will include the SERPS element for the period you worked for them and you will not get that from the state as well.

Public sector final salary pensions – for the Civil Service and local authorities for instance – are fully price inflation-proofed, but not all company pensions *final salary schemes* are. However, the Government now insists that the main benefits payable for the years you are in the scheme after 6 April 1997 must be increased each year in line with inflation, or by 5% if that is less. In practice, some pension schemes might have already given employees such useful benefits for the whole of their service, regardless of this new law – you will need to check what your company does for you.

A **good** final salary scheme will allow your widow/er to have a pension equal to about two-thirds of your own if you die before he/she does. This is a valuable employee benefit. Also a good scheme will pay out a significant lump sum to your widow/er if you die before you retire, and give him/her a pension of two-thirds of what yours would have been.

Another major benefit of a handful of good company pension schemes is that they incorporate *permanent health insurance*, also called income replacement insurance, for their employees. This type of policy may ensure that you will get a proportion of your salary if you have to stop work before your normal retirement age because of illness or a serious accident. When you reach normal retirement age you can start drawing your pension.

SERPS and company pensions

Company pension schemes are allowed to contract-out of the *State Earnings Related Pension Scheme* (SERPS). If they do this, they claim a rebate of some of the *National Insurance contributions* they and their employees make to the Department of Social Security.

The pension scheme invests the money in its own pension fund.

If you belong to a *contracted out* final salary pension scheme, then you cannot also qualify for the SERPS pension during the time you are in the company scheme. SERPS is designed to top up your state pension in relation to your earnings – from £61 to £455 a week (£3,172 to £23,660 a year) for the year 1996/97.

At the moment (1996/97) *final salary schemes* which contract-out must guarantee you a minimum level of pension. They do this by guaranteeing that you will get an equivalent sum to the SERPS pension you would have got if you had stayed in SERPS. This is called the *Guaranteed Minimum Pension* (GMP), and is embedded in your company pension.

But this system of *contracting-out* will change in April 1997. *final salary schemes* will no longer have to pay you a GMP for pensionable service **after** April 1997 but, to be contracted-out, these schemes will have to meet an overall test of quality. This includes inflation-proofing the whole pension each year at least in line with price rises or by 5%, whichever is the lesser. For pension rights earned **before** April 1997, the GMP portion of your pension has to be inflation-proofed for the whole of your life and must now include a spouse's pension right worth half that GMP. The level of inflation-proofing is the Retail Price Index or 5%, whichever is the lower.

The advantages of a final salary scheme

A final salary scheme is usually good value if you expect to stay with the company for most of your working life. A big plus is that the company typically contributes twice as much to it as you do.

Once you are in the scheme they are committed to giving you a certain minimum level of pension, regardless of how much they have in the fund. If they don't have enough in the pension fund they have to pay you out of their annual earnings.

As your pension is related to your length of service and your final salary, you know what you can expect and that your pension will increase in line with your career progress throughout the firm. Therefore the earlier you join the scheme the better, because you will qualify for a bigger pension. This predictability is a major asset when you are planning your retirement. Also, good company pension schemes protect your dependants whether you die the month after retiring or when you are a hundred years old.

If your pension is unlikely to be sufficient, you have time to make alternative plans to top up your retirement income. The following table will help you assess whether you will have enough.

Table 5: Final salary: what you get.

For every £1,000 of your final salary you can expect an annual pension of:

Years in scheme	60ths scheme £	80ths scheme £
1	16.66	12.50
5	83.30	62.50
10	166.60	125.00
15	250.00	187.50
20	333.33	250.00
25	416.60	312.50
30	500.00	375.00
35	583.30	437.50
40	666.66	500.00

This assumes that you do not *commute* any of your pension, ie. take a lump sum in exchange for a smaller pension. (See page 91.)

From **Table 5** you can work out that, if you expect to be in the company's 1/60th scheme for a total of 30 years and are earning £20,000 a year now, you will get a pension of £10,000 at today's figures, unless you take a lesser post. If you get promoted your pension will increase pro rata. If you will be satisfied with £10,000 (at today's figures) plus SERPS (assuming the scheme is not contracted-out), then you have nothing to worry about. However, if you would like a bigger pension then you can make additional arrangements. The simplest way of doing this is by starting an *Additional Voluntary Contribution* (AVC) plan or by investing in *Personal Equity Plans* (PEPs).

AVCs

Every final salary scheme must allow you the facility to have an AVC. You can either choose the plan they offer you or select one of your own. Privately bought AVCs are called *Freestanding AVCs* (FSAVCs). Both types are specifically designed for people in company *final salary schemes*. They work like *personal pensions*. You build up your own private pension fund so that when you retire you use the money to buy an *annuity* (an income for life).

You can contribute as much as you like, provided that the total money you are contributing towards your pension – including your contributions to the company scheme – does not exceed 15% of your normal earnings. That means that if you are already paying 5% to the company scheme, you can invest up to 10% extra. If you are lucky enough to be in a non-contributory pension scheme, then you can invest up to the full 15% in AVCs. Your employer's contributions do not count when calculating your investment ceiling.

Your contributions to the company AVC are paid out of your earnings before tax is deducted. So, if you pay income tax at 24% and your monthly contribution is £50, your take-home pay will be reduced by only £38.00. If you pay 40% tax, your take-home pay will be reduced by only £30.

If, however, you decide to invest in FSAVCs, you pay the contributions less 24% tax. That means that if you want to invest £50 a month, you pay only £38.00. But if you are a higher-rate taxpayer, paying 40% tax, you will have to claim the extra 16%, £8 for every £50, from the Inland Revenue by filling in Form PP120 which is available from your local tax office.

There are four main types of AVC/FSAVC: with-profits; unit-linked; unitised with-profits; and deposit-based:

- With-profit AVCs invest in stocks and shares and property, and each year's gains are locked-in through a *bonus* system, and are considered safer over the distance.

- Unit-linked AVCs invest in unit trust-type funds, and are therefore more volatile and subject to the fluctuations of the stockmarket. If you wish to retire just at the time that the share prices are going through a bad patch, then your final fund will suffer.

- Unitised with-profits are a hybrid of the with-profit and the unit-linked types. They haven't been going well, and overall their track record is not brilliant.

- Deposit-based AVCs only invest in safe and sensible deposit accounts, such as building society funds. They usually offer a poorer return than the others, but are especially suitable for people within five years of retirement, who want a really secure place for their money.

AVCs or FSAVCs?

Whether you buy AVCs through the company scheme or privately depends on a number of factors.

Investment performance: A private FSAVC scheme may offer you a better return because the pension provider you favour has a better track record than the organisation that runs your firm's scheme. However, if the plan you favour is the same as the plan your firm uses, you will usually get better terms by investing in the company scheme. This is because management charges are likely to be less, as the company benefits from bulk sales.

Flexibility: If you already have a *personal pension* but join the company pension scheme, you will be unable to continue contributing to your *personal pension*. But you might be able to convert your *personal pension* into a FSAVC without any penalty. On the other hand, if your new company's AVC scheme is provided by your *personal pension* company, you may be able to convert that into an AVC, and maintain continuity of contributions.

Every year the actuarial firm Bacon & Woodrow conducts a survey of AVCs to establish the best and the worst performers. The table overleaf illustrates the results in the five years to the end of 1995.

Table 6: AVCs best and worst.

£50 a month invested for the five years ended 1 January 1996

Company	Final fund
With-profits plans	
Scottish Mutual*	£4,161
Co-operative Insurance Society (CIS)**	£4,147
Legal & General*	£3,885
Scottish Equitable	£3,837
Prudential	£3,823
Worst: Guardian*	£3,185
Managed unit-linked AVCs	
Fidelity#	£4,406
Scottish Equitable	£4,093
Norwich Union*	£3,974
Gartmore#	£3,954
NPI	£3,946
Worst: Guardian*	£3,620

Notes: * No longer actively marketed
** Only available to employees of Co-operative movement
\# Administration costs excluded

Despite these notes, the table gives you some idea of what you can expect, provided companies keep up their present performance. Past performance is no guarantee of future performance.

Source: 1996 AVC Survey, Bacon & Woodrow.

Another survey, by *Money Management* magazine, looked at the performance of Freestanding AVCs (FSAVCs). See table below:

Table 7: The best and worst FSAVCs.

£100 a month invested for the five years ended 1 November 1995

Company	Final fund
With-profits	
Equitable Life	£7,610
Co-operative Insurance**	£7,554
Scottish Widows	£7,477
NFU Mutual	£7,230
AXA Equity & Law*	£7,148
Worst: MGM*	£6,476
Managed unit-linked FSAVCs	
Morgan Grenfell	£8,825
Fidelity	£8,406
Perpetual	£8,209
Gartmore	£7,955
Professional Managed	£7,791
Worst: Old Mutual	£6,229

Notes: * Unitised with profits
** Only available to employees of Co-operative movement

The final fund is the actual open market option sum you get, after all charges including any penalty for exercising your open market option.

Source: Money Management, February 1996.

Independence: You may prefer to invest privately in a FSAVC, to be independent of the company, to back your own judgement, and even take a bit of a gamble by buying FSAVCs in a more exciting fund rather than those safe and sensible funds on offer through the company.

With an AVC you **must** buy an *annuity* with it at the time you start drawing the company pension; but with a FSAVC you **may** be able to choose your own time to draw it. Normally you should start drawing from your FSAVC at the same time as you start drawing from your company scheme. However, if you change jobs you may have more flexibility if the FSAVC is linked to your new employer's scheme, or if you leave the job you had when you took out the FSAVC, you might want to transfer the fund to a *personal pension*. Then you could be in a position to draw it before you retire, or even leave it to build up to draw on later.

Portability: If you think you may leave the firm to join another one before you retire, you can take your FSAVC plan with you and continue contributing to it. If you have a company AVC, then you will have to leave the money untouched when you go, and buy an *annuity* with it when you retire.

You should not buy AVCs (or FSAVCs) in the highly unlikely event that you may qualify for the full two-thirds final salary pension from your company scheme with the maximum other benefits such as a spouse's pension. The Inland Revenue will not allow you to draw a single penny over the two-thirds limit from your company pension – and that includes AVCs. On the other hand, you may wish to retire early, in which case you are even less likely to breach the two-thirds rule. If you want to top up your pension, you ought to consult the company pensions administrator, to see what size the potential shortfall is likely to be.

There are other reasons for buying AVCs, apart from topping up your pension because you cannot put in enough time to build it up to the full two-thirds final salary permissible. It may be sensible to buy them in order to take the maximum tax-free lump sum from the company pension, while protecting your retirement income.

Also, provided you do not risk busting the two-thirds limit, you can buy AVCs/FSAVCs to build in what is effectively an element of inflation-proofing to your retirement income. You must convert your AVCs into an *annuity* at the same time that you start drawing your company pension: you cannot draw off any tax-free lump sum (unless you started contributing to the AVC before 7 April 1987). Under no circumstances can you draw a lump sum from your FSAVC.

You are never too young to buy AVCs. As it is your own private fund you can put it on ice when you leave the firm or, if it is an FSAVC, you can continue contributing to it when you start your new job, if you join the new employer's pension scheme.

Young people in company schemes are sensibly encouraged to contribute to AVCs while they are 'footloose and fancy free' and not yet committed to the expense of bringing up a young family. They appeal to young high earners who pay tax at the higher rate and are thinking of retiring early.

Disadvantages of final salary schemes

The main disadvantage of a *final salary* scheme is that it usually offers pretty poor value for *early leavers* or job-hoppers. People change jobs for any number of reasons. In certain types of occupation such as publishing, advertising and marketing, motor sales and the leisure industry, high flyers need to change jobs to improve their career prospects and income. Alternatively they may be in industries such as construction and traditionally work on short-term contracts. Redundancy also takes its toll in some cyclical industries and that means that employees have little say in their length of service.

Money purchase schemes

Many companies offer *money purchase* pension schemes instead of *final salary* schemes. A *money purchase* scheme is what is called a 'defined contribution' scheme. This means that you contribute a regular 'defined' sum out of your pay into a pooled fund. Your share of that fund is used to buy you an *annuity* when you retire – but you don't know what your pension is going to be, indeed there are little or no guarantees as to what the ultimate fund will be. A final salary scheme is called a defined benefit scheme because however much you contribute to it hardly matters: the company agrees to pay you a sum related to your salary at the time of retirement and the number of years you have been in the scheme.

Money purchase schemes are similar to *personal pensions* but normally both you **and** your employer contribute to them. The money is invested in a collective fund on your behalf and the ultimate size of your pension depends on how well the investments have performed. Some company *money purchase* schemes also offer valuable *death in service benefits* as an extra. In either case, as with *final salary schemes*, both your contributions and your company's are tax free. Therefore, if you are a standard-rate taxpayer it only costs you £76 to buy £100 worth of contribution. If you pay higher rate tax at 40%, £100 of investment only costs you £60. Put the other way around, for every £100 you invest you will be credited with £131.57 in your pension fund, as a standard-rate taxpayer, or £166.66 if you are paying tax at 40%.

Another tax advantage, as with *final salary schemes*, is that the money in the fund rolls up entirely free of tax compared with most non-pension savings schemes, like unit trusts, where any income earned in the fund (such as dividends from shares) is taxable. *Money purchase* schemes can be contracted-out of SERPS as long as the minimum contribution is made.

When you retire you use the money that has accumulated to buy yourself an *annuity* (income for life). As with *final salary schemes* you are allowed to take some of your funds as a lump sum if you wish, but if you do so, you will get a smaller income, unless you reinvest the lump sum.

The **disadvantage** with *money purchase* schemes is that, unlike *final salary schemes*, you do not know how much pension you are going to get until you retire. You can make an educated guess when you get close to retirement, but cannot be absolutely certain.

Each year the fund managers must send you a statement telling you how much your fund is currently worth and they should give you an idea of what size of pension that would buy you if you continue contributing at the same rate until your normal retirement age. This gives you the opportunity to have an annual pension audit to check whether your retirement fund is building up at a satisfactory rate.

One **advantage** of *money purchase* schemes, as with *final salary schemes*, is that you usually have scope to increase your contributions if you wish to 'buy' a bigger pension. The maximum you can contribute annually to a *money purchase* scheme is 15% of your normal earnings. Anything that your employer contributes does not count against the 15%.

Table 8, below, is a guide to how much pension you can expect from a lump sum based on various *annuity* rates. It is a rough guide because, like mortgage rates, *annuity* rates fluctuate.

Using a rough rule of thumb a man aged 60 who invests £100,000 in an *annuity* may get 10% – which equals £10,000 a year. But if he wants his income to increase annually by 5%, he can expect his initial *annuity* to reduce by something like 42%, to £5,800; a man of 65 who can get a level *annuity* paying 12% (£12,000 a year), and who wants his income to increase by 5% a year, can expect his pension to reduce by about 36%, and his initial income will therefore be £6,400. You must remember that these figures are only a guide. You can only be certain of what pension you will get for your fund at the time you actually buy your *annuity*.

Table 8: Money purchase pensions.

Converting your money purchase funds into a pension income. How big a fund will you need?

To achieve an annual income for life of	8.5%	Annuity rates 10%	12.5%
£ 5,000	£ 58,000	£ 50,000	£ 40,000
£10,000	£117,600	£100,000	£ 80,000
£15,000	£176,400	£150,000	£120,000
£20,000	£234,000	£200,000	£160,000

Another advantage of *money purchase* schemes is that if you leave the firm before you retire, ie. you become an *early leaver*, you may not lose out as badly as you do with a final salary scheme. You have the choice of leaving the money in the fund until you retire, in which case it will keep on growing, or you can transfer it to your new employer's scheme (if the employer will accept it). In either case your money will keep on growing for you. What you cannot do is take the money and run.

It is easy for the employer you are leaving to work out how much you are owed, because it is a defined share of the total fund. This can be paid direct into your new scheme, probably with a modest deduction for charges and expenses.

Group personal pensions

Some small firms offer their employees the opportunity to invest in *group personal pensions* which are also similar to *personal pensions*. They are totally portable and you can take your fund with you if you leave early. The advantage of belonging to them, as opposed to contributing to your own *personal pension*, is that it is usually cheaper because the company gets a discount off the charges because more than one person, typically a minimum of five employees, is involved. Also, the company is often prepared to contribute to it on your behalf – pound for pound, or better – so your fund builds up faster than an individual *personal pension* would grow.

Hybrid pension schemes

Some employers offer a scheme which involves elements of both final salary and a *money purchase* scheme. The idea is to offer a pension that bears some relation to earnings and which does not penalise the early leaver too badly. In a hybrid scheme the contributions of both employee and employer are shared between two funds. One fund is a *money purchase* fund and the other fund is insured and builds up separately. The two together guarantee the employee a salary-related pension based on, say, 100ths, so that for every year the employee is in the scheme he is guaranteed a pension of 100th of his final salary.

How much does joining the company scheme cost you?

Your contributions are eligible for tax relief, which means that for every £1 you contribute as a basic-rate taxpayer (24%), your take-home pay is only reduced by 76p. If the scheme is contracted-out of SERPS you will pay reduced *National Insurance contributions*, if you currently pay the full rate. Your basic state pension will not be affected, but your future SERPS pension will be absorbed into the company scheme.

Early leavers

Final salary pension schemes are designed for long-stayers who will remain in the same company until retirement. These schemes are not geared up for mobile workforces and they penalise participants if they leave after a couple of years or so, although pension legislation is forcing employers to be fairer to *early leavers*. If you are in a final salary scheme for less than two years, you are not entitled to anything more than a return of your own contributions – not even the contributions your firm has made on your behalf. This is particularly damaging to people who join a non-contributory pension scheme and leave before being a member for two years, because they get nothing back and have lost the opportunity to make any pension provision for themselves! But they could take out a *personal pension* and take advantage of the carry back/carry forward rules. Those who do get their money back will receive it in cash less a special flat rate of 20% (1996/97) and that cannot be claimed back even if they are non-taxpayers.

If the scheme has contracted out of SERPS, there will probably be a hefty deduction which the company will pay to the DSS to buy back your rights for the state top-up scheme for the time you were employed. You do not usually get any interest on the money you receive – though some companies will give you some. So, overall, the return on your money is pretty dismal.

If you have put in **more than two years** you cannot draw the cash, as such, but you don't lose it. You have four main options. You can:

- Accept a deferred pension.
- Arrange to transfer your pension rights to your new employer's pension scheme.
- Buy a *deferred annuity* (a buy-out policy).
- Transfer the money into your own special *personal pension*.

Deferred pension

The company must offer you the right to a *deferred pension* which you can draw at retirement age. However, the deferred pension is based on the number of years that you were in the pension scheme, your salary on leaving the firm, and whether the scheme was based on 60ths or 80ths. At its simplest, this means that if you are earning £15,000 when you leave the company's scheme at age 35, after six years in the scheme which is based on 80ths, and your normal retirement age is 65, you will be entitled to a pension of £1,125 in 30 years' time (£15,000 x 6/80). However, for anyone leaving the company after 1 January 1991, this figure must be at least partly inflation-proofed, either by the Retail Price Index or 5%, whichever is the lower.

If the scheme is contracted-out of SERPS then, alas, the position will be much more complicated. Your company scheme booklet will fill in the details. The disadvantage is that a deferred pension does not take into account any future pay increases (which tend to exceed prices inflation) so it will be based on your earnings at whatever level you had achieved by the time you left.

Example:

Twins Peter and Paul who each earn £20,000 are due to retire this year from the same firm. Paul has had four jobs and has always joined his company's final salary scheme and will get deferred pensions from the first three. Peter has worked with the same firm for 40 years, during which time he has been in the final salary pension scheme. All schemes are based on 80ths and have not contracted-out of SERPS. Peter's company pension will be £6,000 a year more than Paul's. Why?

Table 9: Effect of job-hopping on final salary schemes

	No. of years in scheme	Leaving salary	Pension	Calculation
Peter	40	£20,000	**£10,000.00**	£20,000 × 40/80
Paul	Job 1 10	£ 500	£ 62.50	£ 50 × 10/80
	Job 2 10	£ 2,000	£ 250.00	£ 2,000 × 10/80
	Job 3 10	£10,000	£ 1,250.00	£10,000 × 10/80
	Job 4 10	£20,000	£ 2,500.00	£20,000 × 10/80
Paul's total pension			**£ 4,062.50**	

NB: For simplicity this example assumes that none of the schemes offered any inflation-proofing, though now the pension for anyone who leaves the company after 1 January 1991 must be increased by the Retail Price Index or 5%, whichever is the lower.

If we recast the figures assuming that Paul's pension schemes all offered 5% inflation since before he left his first job, we see that his ultimate pension score improves by £1,407 a year to £5,469 – which is still £4,531 less than his twin brother!

Table 10: Effect of job-hopping on a final salary pension (inflation-proofing old pensions)

		No. of years in scheme	Leaving salary	Pension without inflation-proofing	Deferred pension increased by 5% pa
Peter		40	£20,000	**£10,000.00**	—
Paul	Job 1	10	£ 500	£ 62.50	£ 270
	Job 2	10	£ 2,000	£ 250.00	£ 663
	Job 3	10	£10,000	£1,250.00	£2,036
	Job 4	10	£20,000	£2,500.00	£2,500
Paul's total pension				**£4,062.50**	**£5,469**

You can take it with you when you go

When you leave one employer to join another, you have a number of options:

– you can transfer your pension rights from the old scheme into the scheme run by your present employers, if they will accept it and if you are likely to stay long enough to make it worthwhile;

– you can ask for the money to be paid into a *personal pension* or a special type of *personal pension* of your own, known as a *Buy-out plan* (often called a Section 32 plan).

Until recently the rules said that only people who left a previous employer's service **after** 1 January 1986 had the right to transfer their benefits to a new company pension scheme, provided the new employer has a suitable scheme; employees had no legal rights to transfer their funds if they left before 1986. However, that has changed: the 1995 Pensions Act extended this right to most people who left a previous employer's scheme at any time **before** 1986. Exceptions include schemes which fully protect pre-1986 early leaver benefits against inflation. In these circumstances, your right to take a transfer will continue to be at the scheme's discretion.

If your new employer has a suitable scheme which you can join, and if he is prepared to accept a transfer value, you will be offered one of the following:

- some extra years of pensionable service; effectively you are buying in some extra years and the scheme will assume that you have been in it for longer than you really have (it won't be the same number of years that you put into your previous scheme, inevitably it will be fewer), **or**
- a specified annual amount of pension payable on retirement or death (which will not vary with changes in your pay), **or**
- a *group money purchase* pension, which is a type of personal pension in which you build up a fund from which to buy your pension later, and which is not related to your final salary or the number of years' service you have put in.

Transfer values

What happens if you want to take it with you when you go? When you leave a company and have been in the final salary scheme for more than two years, you can ask to transfer your pension. You inquire about this as soon as you know you are leaving. The employers you are leaving must give you information which includes details of a *transfer value* which should equal the pension rights that you are sacrificing by moving on. Their *actuary* calculates the transfer value by taking into account your leaving salary, length of service and any benefits you are giving up such as a spouse's pension.

In basic terms, the *actuary* works out how much money you would need to invest today to ensure you get the level of benefits on retirement which you have already qualified for. In turn, this transfer value is translated into cash which the scheme pays over to your new employer's pension scheme. In effect you are using the money to add some of the past years of service with your previous employer to those you will be putting in with your new employer. In practice, if you proceed with the transfer, you will probably lose a year or so in the process unless both employers belong to the same 'transfer club' and have a reciprocal deal which protects your pension.

How to go about it

Before deciding to transfer your pension to your new employers you should find out what rights you have in the old scheme, and check whether any of these rights will continue to be provided after you leave the company. For instance:

- Will the old pension be a fixed amount, or will it increase each year until retirement by, say, 5%?

- Will the old pension be guaranteed for a minimum period (normally five years) so that if you die within five years of retirement your spouse or dependants continue getting the pension or at least some of it for the rest of the five years, or a lump sum?

- When you die, will your surviving spouse have a pension, say half of your pension or even two-thirds?
- What benefits will there be if you die before retirement, such as a widow/er's pension or lump sum?

You then need to check what benefits you will get in the new scheme in order to make sensible comparisons. As this is often rather complicated, it would be sensible to ask your trade union officials, if they understand these matters, or an independent financial adviser who specialises in pension transfers.

You should also think about looking up the benefits you have acquired in previous company pension schemes you have been a member of, and tidying up your pension rights in one move. This could enhance the benefits you get in the new scheme. But you will have to go through the same process, described above, for each transfer. This is rather time consuming.

Before committing yourself to the new company's pension scheme, you could also consider getting your old company's pension transferred to your very own pension fund. If you do this you have the choice of either a Section 32 *Buy-out plan*, which is technically a *deferred annuity*, or a *personal pension* plan (for full details see next chapter). *buy-out plans* were introduced in 1981 and have special benefits for people with a particularly large amount to transfer, and who were in a *contracted-out* final salary company pension scheme. They cover the *Guaranteed Minimum Pension* (GMP) – or the SERPS part of your pension – as well as investing the rest of your money to enhance your ultimate fund. Pension companies will only accept the transfer if they are sure the sum is sufficient.

You cannot add any new money to a buy-out plan, so if you don't wish to join your new employer's pension scheme and you want to continue contributing to your own pension plan, you will have to start a separate *personal pension*. This is easy enough and nothing to worry about. If anything, it might be more convenient to have two types of private pension because it will give you more flexibility later on. One problem with a buy-out plan is that you will not be able to trade it in for an *annuity* until the retirement date set by your original employers. You can potentially get round this by transferring the funds, later, to a *personal pension*.

If, however, at the time you leave the company you wish to transfer the money to a *personal pension*, then you have various other points to consider. If your scheme was *contracted-out* of SERPS, the *personal pension* will not guarantee that the GMP will be paid, but you can take the chance of investing your money to obtain a better benefit. If the *personal pension* is contracted-out, you will have to forgo any rights to SERPS, or to GMP, for the time you are contributing to it, because you will be taking the money from the DSS to pay into your *personal pension*. You will need to be confident that the pension company investment managers can give you a better return than SERPS, which only keeps up with price inflation.

If your *personal pension* is not *contracted-out*, ie. you are not partly funding it with your National Insurance rebate, you will continue to qualify for SERPS. You can transfer your money from the old scheme into a *personal pension* and at the same time join your new employer's pension scheme. However, if you choose this option, you cannot add any new money to your *personal pension*. You can't belong to a company pension scheme **and** contribute to a *personal pension* at the same time, unless you can take advantage of the *carry-back* rules.

An important disadvantage of transferring your company

pension rights into your own *personal pension* or buy-out plan, if you are moving to another employer, is that *personal pensions* differ from most employers' schemes and don't normally provide the same range of benefits – such as provision for your dependants when you die. You can, though, pay extra to get these benefits added, or settle for a smaller pension.

Another disadvantage is that *personal pension* schemes invest the money paid into them until you retire, when you must use the proceeds to buy a pension – but you cannot be sure until you retire what your pension will be. So you could be swapping a known pension for an unknown pension. *personal pensions* generally have far higher administration costs than employers' schemes and *personal pension* salesmen are normally entitled to commission. Both of these have to come out of your transfer value. So once these have been paid, it is unlikely that what is left will buy you, on day one, a higher pension than you started with.

In view of all these problems, it is essential that you get professional advice before arranging any transfers.

Opting out of a company pension scheme

If you are a member of a company pension scheme you have an **absolute** right to opt out, even if you stay with the company. You may, usually unwisely, not want to be in a pension scheme at all, or you may – more commonly – wish to be independent and buy yourself a *personal pension* instead. Alternatively, you may be eligible to join the company scheme and yet want to make *personal pension* arrangements instead.

Should you do this?

If you are a member of your employer's pension scheme, it is nearly always best to stay a member; and if you are eligible, or will be eligible, it is nearly always best for you to join.

The main reasons are:

- Few employers will contribute to a *personal pension*, so you may stand to lose very valuable employer's contributions if you take out a *personal pension*. Typically employers contribute 10% of your pay into their scheme, compared with the 5% you would normally contribute.

- A *personal pension* is unlikely to provide you with better benefits than your employer's scheme, especially if the employer makes no contribution to it.

- You will be paying the expenses of setting up your own scheme.

The financial services watchdog, the Securities & Investments Board, which has had all sorts of trouble with pensions companies who persuaded employees to opt out of company pensions to buy *personal pensions*, has issued some guidelines to employees wishing to do their own pension thing. You can get a copy from their office. It suggests:

If you are staying with your employer but are thinking of leaving the pension scheme to buy a personal pension, ask the employer the following questions:

- Will your employer contribute to your *personal pension*?

- If you leave your employer's scheme can you rejoin later?

- If you leave the scheme will you be entitled to any benefits offered by the scheme – ie. life assurance cover, dependants' pension or disability benefit? (If not, you will have to buy these for yourself.)

If your employer answers **NO** to any of these questions you should think very carefully before deciding to opt out. You should also check with your employer exactly what benefits you are entitled to. Remember: the trustees of your employer's pension scheme are legally required to provide you with information on the benefits you may get from the pension scheme.

If you are eligible to join the employer's scheme in future, but are currently in a waiting period, it is probably best to wait. You do not have to take out a *personal pension*. There are other ways of saving while you wait.

What happens when you retire from the company?

Four months before you retire from the company, the Department of Social Security should automatically write and tell you how much state pension you can expect. However, at least six months before you retire, you should ask your employers (and your FSAVC supplier, if you have bought an AVC privately), how much pension you should get from them.

Different rules apply depending on whether you are in a *final salary* scheme or a *money purchase* scheme:

If you are in a *final salary* scheme you should ask:

- What is the maximum pension you have qualified for?

THE COMPLETE GUIDE TO PERSONAL PENSIONS

- What is the maximum lump sum you could get if you *commute* the pension, by sacrificing some pension income, and what size pension will this leave you with?

(For a comparison, you could also ask what pension you would get if you took only half the available lump sum.)

If you are married, ask:

- What will your spouse's pension be if you die before he/she does? Typically it will be two-thirds of your own pension.

If there is no automatic provision for a spouse's pension, you should ask:

- Do you have the option of accepting a reduced pension for yourself in favour of arranging for a spouse's pension? If so, ask for the figures, both before and after *commutation*.

If you are in a *money purchase* scheme, your fund will be used to buy you an *annuity*, so you should ask:

- How much money is in your fund?
- What is the maximum lump sum you can expect if you *commute* part of it?
- What size *annuity* you can expect:

    a) if you don't *commute* your pension;

    b) if you do *commute* it.
- Can you transfer your money and buy an *annuity* from the company of your own choice? If so, will they penalise you, and, if so, by how much?

Armed with this information, you should be in a position to make some decisions, but in Chapter 7 we go into detail as to whether or not to *commute* your pension. We also explain the various types of *annuity* that are available to employees in *money purchase* schemes, whether company schemes or *personal pensions*.

What happens when you die?

If you die **before** your normal retirement age without having started to draw your company pension, your dependants **may** be entitled to a lump-sum payment of anything up to four times your salary at death, regardless of how many years you have been in the pension scheme.

The company may refund all of your contributions, with or without interest, and a pension equal to two-thirds of your pension (ie. 4/9ths of your normal salary) as well. Further, if you have any children under 16, they may be entitled to a pension until they are 16.

This money doesn't necessarily come out of the employer's pension fund. It is more likely to come from an insurance company, if the company has suitable insurance, and therefore employees in *money purchase* schemes may also qualify for this arrangement. But you will need to check with your employers – just because you are in a pension scheme does not mean that full *death in service benefits* are available.

If *death in service benefits* are available, the trustees of the pension scheme usually have the discretion to decide the destination of the money. But it is wise, if you are in such a scheme, for you to inform the trustees of where you would like the money to go if you do die prematurely. You fill in an expression of wish form. This is especially sensible if you want to benefit a partner to whom you are not married. It could save delays and financial stress if he/she is reliant on your earnings.

If your employer does not run a death in service scheme, then your dependants may just get a lump sum equivalent to a refund of your and your employer's contributions with or without interest added. If you are in a *money purchase* scheme, your beneficiaries may be entitled to the value of your fund at your death. This will be limited to four times annual salary as a lump sum (together with a refund of personal contributions and growth). The rest must provide a widow/er's and/or dependant's pension.

If you are in a *final salary* scheme, and you die **after** retiring, then your spouse (or your partner if you have signed the expression of wish in his/her favour) may be entitled to continue getting two-thirds of your pension until he or she dies. But if you are in a *money purchase* scheme, then it will depend on the type of *annuity* you bought with your pension fund (see Chapter 7 for details about selecting an *annuity*).

Checklist for people in company pension schemes

How good is your company *final salary* scheme?

The **perfect** scheme would be one that:

- Gives you a **full** two-thirds final salary pension after a maximum of 20 years.

- Is based on total earnings, such as personal use of a company car and free private medical cover (like BUPA) – not just basic pay.

- Gives you a **fully inflation-proofed** pension.
- Does not include the basic state pension in its calculations (ie. the scheme doesn't 'pretend' to be more generous than it is).
- Is not contracted-out of SERPS – leaving you with the state top-up scheme as well.
- Includes a two-thirds pension for permanent incapacity before retirement, increasing by 5% each year.
- Includes a lump sum equal to at least four times salary for your widow/er or partner if you die **before** drawing your pension.
- Includes a pension of two-thirds of pay for widow/er for death **after** retirement, plus a pension for any dependant children until they are 18 or finish full-time education.
- Offers generous arrangements for *early leavers*.

However, there are few of these around. In the real world, you can count yourself lucky if you get half these features!

How good is your company *money purchase* scheme?

- It says it will try to match the benefits of a final salary scheme, as listed above, but it won't be able to guarantee these.
- The employer will pay at least half the contributions, which typically will range from 6% to 16.5% of your normal earnings.
- Your investments will be managed by a leading fund manager with a good track record in the pensions market.

- You won't have any financial penalties if you become an early leaver for whatever reason, including early retirement, or you want to reduce or stop your contributions.
- It should offer you a disability pension if you become unable to work through sickness or injury.

Reading list

For further information on company pensions write to the National Association of Pension Funds, 12-18 Grosvenor Gardens, London SW1W 0DH. Their range of leaflets include:

Early Retirement: How it affects your pension
Pension Transfers: How to decide
Leaving your job and keeping your pension
Women and the risks of retirement
Retirement: A risky business
Early Retirement: How it affects your pension
New job? It may pay more than you think
Changing your job? Opting out of a pension scheme? What about your pension?

Chapter 4:
Personal pensions

About half the working population are in jobs which do not offer them the chance to join a company pension scheme. They therefore need to take charge of their own retirement income planning. The launch of *personal pensions* on 1 July 1988 was a major watershed for them. This was heralded by the media and industry alike as a major revolution. It was not that the product itself was revolutionary, indeed it was developed from the old self-employed pensions, going under the formidably-named *Retirement Annuity Policies* (RAPs), which are no longer available to newcomers. What was new was that employed people were actively encouraged to buy them. Employees now knew they had the choice: being locked into an unsuitable company pension (if, indeed, one was available and open to them); or buying their very own portable pension, to which they could contribute regardless of their employers.

The *personal pension* is in many ways an investor's dream. It is one of the most tax-efficient long-term savings products available. It gives employees – and the self-employed – the opportunity to make regular savings, net of standard rate (24%) income tax, to produce a lump sum with which to buy an income on retirement. Higher-rate taxpayers can claw back 40% tax.

The savings within the plan are not taxed, unlike many other forms of savings, so the fund grows faster, and when you retire you have the chance, subject to existing tax rules, to take some 25% of the money as a tax-free sum. Anyone, even non-taxpayers, not in a company pension scheme, and who has not yet reached 75, can invest in a *personal pension*.

The idea is that you can build up a *personal pension* fund throughout your working life regardless of how many different companies you work for. When you decide to retire (it must be by age 75) you can use your savings to produce an income for life. How much you have in your fund depends on two things: how much you invest, and how well you have invested it. Obviously, the earlier you start, the more your fund has the chance to grow.

The *personal pension* has many advantages:

– You can choose how much you want to invest and you can vary your premiums.

– Your contributions are eligible for tax relief at your highest rate, and you can make use of unused tax relief in respect of unused relief for previous years (see **Table 13**, page 102).

– Your pension fund rolls up tax free.

-- If you are employed you can currently claim a rebate from your *National Insurance contributions* (via the Department of Social Security) by *contracting-out* of the *State Earnings Related Pension Scheme* (SERPS) and add that money to your own contributions.

PERSONAL PENSIONS

- Your employer may be persuaded to contribute as well.
- It is portable; you can take it with you when you change jobs or become self-employed (and vice versa).
- You can start drawing from it at any time you want to after the age of 50 instead of having to wait for the state retirement age.
- You can draw a lump sum from it when you start drawing your pension.
- If you already have an old-style *personal pension* Retirement Annuity Policy in your investment portfolio you can add a *personal pension* to give you extra flexibility.
- If you are in a company scheme and also have earnings from another source, then you can use these earnings as a basis for your own *personal pension*.
- You can choose how the money is invested.
- You can add life cover and get tax relief on the premiums you pay.

In this chapter we will look at each merit.

Paying contributions

You can decide how much you want to pay and when you want to pay your contributions. You can choose to have a regular savings plan and pay monthly or annually; you can choose whether to make a lump-sum investment whenever you choose, within the limits set by the Inland Revenue.

If you decide to pay regular amounts monthly or annually, your pension company can arrange for you to build in provision for annual increases in your contributions so they keep pace with the anticipated increases in your earnings. This is quite important because your fund will grow faster and, as you get older, your pay is likely to increase above the level of inflation. Besides, your standard of living is likely to improve as you get older and most people like to maintain a similar lifestyle when they retire.

You will probably discover that what seemed an adequate target when you started your plan does not look quite so good later on – alas the goalposts appear to move as your quality of lifestyle increases. It is therefore important to review your pension plan every year or so to ensure that you are on course. You may prefer to contribute to your pension fund every so often, perhaps when you get a profit share from your employers or windfall money. Indeed, if you are self-employed and your earnings are irregular, this option will give you the flexibility you require.

Even if you start off with a regular payment plan, most good companies will allow you to add single contributions from time to time. The best companies will allow you to vary your payment patterns without any penalty. You can increase, decrease, stop or restart your contributions, almost at will. This facility is helpful for a number of reasons: for example, if you have a career break to bring up the children or to look after a sick relation, you do not have to worry about keeping up your contributions while you are not earning; or, if you are approaching retirement or are temporarily earning extra cash, then you might want to syphon some more income into your plan.

The Government encourages older people, especially, to increase their contributions as they get closer to retirement by allowing them to increase their tax-free contributions.

Alternatively, if you are currently employed, you might become unemployed, perhaps through redundancy or illness; or if you are self-employed a major contract may fall through and leave you unable to keep up your payments. On the other hand, you might take a job which offers a really great pension scheme. In any of these cases you can arrange with the insurance company to stop contributing to your *personal pension* and leave the money invested. Naturally, it won't be as good as if you had kept up the payments, but you do not lose the gains made and the chance for further gains. Then, if you find that you can afford to restart your contributions, you can usually do so. However, you should check that the insurance company will allow you this flexibility before you start your plan.

Tax relief on contributions

If you are **employed,** your contributions are paid net of basic-rate tax. So if you are a standard-rate taxpayer (24%), for every £100 you contribute you are credited with £131.57 which goes straight into your pension fund. This is easily done because the insurance company reclaims the tax from the Inland Revenue. If, however, you pay higher-rate tax at 40% then you are credited with £131.57 for every £100 you invest, and have to claim the other 16% (£21.05) direct from the Inland Revenue using form PP120.

If you are **self-employed** or a partner (in a business sense) slightly different rules apply: you claim your contributions against tax at your highest rate of tax by submitting Form PP120 with your annual tax return, or getting your accountant to do it.

The Inland Revenue annually reviews the maximum contributions that taxpayers can pay at different ages into their *personal pension*. These percentages are different from those for people still contributing to the old-style self-employed *Retirement Annuity Plans*, which could not be started after 30 June 1988. However, people who are still contributing to the old-style plans can contribute the difference to a personal pension, provided they are aged 36 or more.

Table 11: Maximum contributions allowable against tax, 1996/97

% of net relevant earnings#

Age*	Personal pension – new style	Retirement annuity – old style	Allowance available to Section 226## holders for personal pension
35 or under	17.5%	17.5%	nil
36-45	20.0%	17.5%	2.5%
46-50	25.0%	17.5%	7.5%
51-55	30.0%	20.0%	10.0%
56-60	35.0%	22.5%	12.5%
61-74	40.0%	27.5%	12.5%
75+	nil	nil	nil
Life cover**	5.0%	5.0%	n/a

* Age at start of tax year (6 April).
** Included in the above percentages (see Life Cover, page 120).
\# For employees net relevant earnings are all normal earnings; and for the self-employed they are taxable earnings, ie. earnings less expenses.
\#\# Section 226 policies are also called Retirement Annuity Plans.

These figures are correct, provided your earnings are below the *earnings cap* (see below).

Whether you are employed or self-employed, there is another, overriding restriction on how much you can contribute to a *personal pension*. This is something known as the *earnings cap*, also known as the *pensions cap*. This is set annually in the Budget and is expected to increase more or less in line with inflation. The pensions cap for 1996/97 is £82,200 (it was £78,600 in 1995/96). This means, for example, that the maximum that 51 to 55-year-olds can contribute to their *personal pension*, in 1996/97, is £16,440 (£82,200 x 20%). In cash terms, the maximum contributions you are allowed to make to a *personal pension* each year are illustrated in the table below:

Table 12: Maximum sum you can contribute to *personal pensions* each year

Age at start of tax year	% of net relevant earnings	Pension cap
35 or under	17.5%	£14,385
36-45	20.0%	£16,440
46-50	25.0%	£20,550
51-55	30.0%	£24,660
56-60	35.0%	£28,770
61-75	40.0%	£32,880

Note: For employees, net relevant earnings are normal earnings. For the self-employed, they are net profit (earnings less expenses).

Unused relief

If you want to make extra contributions you can use the unused portion of your allowance from the previous six years, on top of your contributions for the current year.

Example:

When Andrew Baxter left the firm he was working with in March 1993, he was 45 and, as his new employer didn't have a pension scheme, he decided to start a *personal pension* (not contracted-out) that year. He has made his maximum contribution of £5,000 this year, but he has some spare cash, and he wants to use up his unused relief from previous years. This is how to work out how much he is entitled to contribute:

Table 13: How to work out unused tax relief

Tax year	Age	Earnings limits £	Tax relief %	Max allowable contributions £	Actual contributions £	Unused relief £
1993/94	45	15,000	20%	3,000	2,000	1,000
1994/95	46	16,000	25%	4,000	2,500	1,500
1995/96	47	18,000	25%	4,500	4,000	500
1996/97	48	20,000	25%	5,000	5,000	—
Andrew can contribute an extra						**3,000**

If Andrew wants to contribute an extra £1,500 he has to wipe the slate clean for the earliest years of unused relief first. This means he uses the £1,000 unused relief for 1993/94 first. This leaves him with £500 which comes from the following tax year, 1994/95. He then has a 'spare' £500 from 1994/95 which he must use before the year 2001/2002 or lose it forever.

SERPS rebate

SERPS is the *State Earnings Related Pension Scheme*, which is paid as a top-up to your *basic state pension*. If you are **employed** and earning more than £60.99 a week (£3,171.48 a year), and are not in a contracted-out company pension scheme, you and your employers are already paying for your SERPS pension, whether you know it or not. One part of your *National Insurance contributions* qualifies you for a *basic state pension*, and another part qualifies you for a SERPS pension. However, under certain circumstances, you can arrange to get your SERPS contributions rebated into your own special type of private pension. There are two types:

- *Appropriate Personal Pension* (APP). This is a personal pension plan into which you ask the DSS to pay your SERPS rebate. The idea is that at retirement your pension at least equals the SERPS pension you have given up. But you should seriously consider topping it up with extra contributions.

- *Contracted-out money purchase pension* (COMP) is similar to an APP but is set up by employers for their staff. The company must make some contribution to it.

Diverting your NI contributions in this way is called *contracting-out*, and does not affect your basic state pension in the least.

The idea behind a personal SERPS pension (whether an APP or a COMP) is that if you divert some of your *National Insurance contributions* into your own pension plan now, the state doesn't have to pay you a SERPS pension covering the period you have been opted out, when you retire. You have to make the decision whether the insurance company of your choice can do better than the state.

A SERPS rebate *personal pension* can be an attractive facility for younger people, in particular the better paid, and for men aged up to about 45 and women aged up to 40. Young people in their late teens or early twenties have the most to gain from such a pension scheme with a good insurance company, because their fund has longer to grow.

Before going into the nitty-gritty of buying a 'rebate only' SERPS pension in your own right, it is vital to understand the basic concept of SERPS. It is important to remember that the state pension comes in two main bites (ignoring Graduated Pensions which are not relevant for anyone young enough to be interested in setting up a SERPS pension).

- The basic state pension which is currently (1996/97) £61.15 a week (£3,179.80 year), plus an allowance for a spouse which is currently £1,903.20 a year.

- SERPS, the State Earnings Related Pension, which has been related to part of your earnings since 1978.

Both of these pensions are **price** inflation-proofed – as opposed to **earnings** inflation-proofed, which is usually higher – and can be expected to hold most of their buying power. The basic decision on whether to opt out of SERPS depends on whether you are convinced that your favoured insurance company will offer you a better return for your money in the long term than the state.

You qualify for the basic state pension from the *National Insurance contributions* you make. As soon as your earnings are £61 a week (1996/97) you must pay 2% on all earnings up to that £61, regardless of whether you are in any personal pension or company scheme, and then 10% on all of your earnings between £61 and £455 a week.

On top of that, currently (1996/97) **you** pay for your SERPS pension out of 1.8% of any earnings in the 'band' between £61 a week (£3,172 a year) and £455 a week (£23,660 a year), and your employer contributes 3% on the same 'band' of earnings. Therefore:

- if you are earning £100 a week, you pay 70p a week to SERPS;
- if you are earning £300 a week (£15,600 a year), you pay £4.30 a week; and
- if you are earning £455 or more, you pay £7.10.

Now **add** to that 3% of your earnings between £61 and £455 a week that your employers have to contribute to National Insurance towards your SERPS pension (unless they have contracted-out):

- if you are earning £100 a week your employer pays £1.17 a week;
- If you are earning £300 a week your employer pays £7.17 a week; and
- if you are earning £455 or more a week your employer pays £11.82 a week.

When you add the two payments together, you have the total that you can claim back from the DSS to contribute to a *personal pension* in your own right. On top of that, for the year 1996/97 people aged 30 or more are given an incentive *bonus* of

THE COMPLETE GUIDE TO PERSONAL PENSIONS

1% of band earnings to encourage them to contract-out of SERPS. The following table illustrates the amount that employees under 30 can claim for their *personal pension*:

Table 14: How much can you claim from your National Insurance contributions to pay into a contracted-out personal pension?

Your annual earnings	Annual contributions Yours	Employer's	Total	Total including tax relief
£10,000	£122.90	£204.84	£327.74	£ 366.66
£15,000	£212.90	£354.75	£567.65	£ 635.16
£20,000	£302.90	£504.84	£807.74	£ 903.66
£23,660+	£368.78	£614.64	£975.42	£1,100.20

The rebate also includes tax relief on the individual's share – ie. 5.37% of band earnings.

That results in quite a lot of money. If you are earning £20,000 a year, you will be paying £302.90 a year and your employer will be paying £504.84, which adds up to £807.74. It will be even more for people aged 30 and over, because they qualify for an extra 1% of band earnings. You can use this money to buy a *personal pension*, and build up your own pension fund. The money is rebated by the DSS direct to your chosen pension provider as a lump sum at the end of the tax year.

As from 6 April 1997, however, the rules change somewhat. In order to encourage more people to become independent of the state and contract-out of SERPS – and to stay contracted-out – the Government is increasing the size of the rebate for older people. The rebates for younger people will be lower than for older people because younger people have more time to grow enough to fund a pension of equivalent value to SERPS, which these pensions replace. The new rebates are intended to ensure that most people with this type of pension should not need to switch back into SERPS.

The SERPS changes

As far as *final salary* schemes are concerned, there will be a flat-rate rebate of 4.6% of 'band earnings' for the tax year 1997/1998. This will be split 3.0% for the employer and 1.6% for the employee (compared with 3% and 1.8% at present), but the employer must take full responsibility for the *Guaranteed Minimum Pension* (GMP) part (see Chapter 3).

As far as *Appropriate Personal Pensions* (APPs) are concerned, the total rebate will be age-related, starting at 3.4% of band earnings (currently, 1996/97, those between £61 and £455 a week) for people aged 15, to 9% for people aged 46 and over.

As far as *contracted-out money purchase schemes* (COMPS) – the company sponsored version of APPs – are concerned, the age-related rebate will start at 3.1% for people aged 15 and rise to 9% for those aged 47 and over.

Table 15: Sample APP and COMPS rebates as from 6 April 1997

Age	APP rebate	COMPS rebate
15	3.4%	3.1%
20	3.6%	3.4%
25	3.9%	3.6%
30	4.2%	3.9%
32	4.3%	4.0%
34	4.4%	4.2%
36	4.7%	4.5%
38	5.0%	4.8%
40	5.4%	5.2%
41	5.6%	5.4%
42	6.0%	5.8%
43	6.7%	6.4%
44	7.4%	7.2%
45	8.2%	8.0%
46	9.0%	8.9%
47+	9.0%	9.0%

(Note: the difference in percentages is technical, due to the differing expenses of the different contracts.)

Using the earnings bands that are currently in force – £61 to £455 a week (earnings between £3,172 and £23,660 a year), the changes are illustrated in the table overleaf.

Table 16: Effect of the changes in the *SERPS* rebate available, as from April 1997

Age	Total annual *SERPS* contributions available as rebate for APP on earnings of £15,000 (ignoring tax relief)		
	1996/97	1997/98*	Difference
	£	£	£
15	567.65	402.15	- 165.50
20	567.65	425.80	- 141.85
30	567.65	496.77	- 70.88
40	567.65	638.71	+ 71.06
41	567.65	662.36	+ 94.71
42	567.65	709.68	+ 142.03
43	567.65	792.47	+ 224.82
44	567.65	875.27	+ 307.62
45	567.65	969.89	+ 402.24
46	567.65	1,064.52	+ 496.87

* Assuming same £11,828 band earnings as 1996/97 (ie. £3,172-£15,000).

If you are in a company pension scheme which has not *contracted-out* you are still allowed to contract-out of SERPS personally and run your own *Appropriate Pension Plan* alongside the company scheme. However, the system is probably more use to employed people who are not in any company scheme, and who are prepared to contribute extra from their own earnings. In fact it is vital that at some stage you do top it up, but starting a contracted-out SERPS pension does get you started on your pension planning.

Should YOU contract-out of SERPS?

Your decision must depend on your:

- attitude to the risk involved
- age
- earning potential
- health

If you are a **pessimist** and very cautious, and on the basis that a bird in the hand is worth two in the bush, you are better staying with SERPS. By choosing this option you must accept that your ultimate earnings-related pension is decreasing in buying power. However, if you are an **optimist** and believe that your chosen pension provider can consistently increase your fund by 4% (or more than inflation) each year, then you should seriously consider contracting out.

Your **age** comes into the equation too. The younger you are the better off you are likely to be in *contracting-out* of SERPS, because the ultimate pension you can expect from SERPS will get lower from the year 2000. You will also have more time for your *personal pension* to build up.

It has long been broadly accepted that, depending on salary, women aged 38-43 and men aged 44-48 who have already contracted-out of SERPS, should seriously consider contracting back in again. But, in the light of the new regime starting April 1997, the ground rules have changed. On the Government *Actuary's* assumptions, the outcome of investing the rebate in a *personal pension* as from April 1997-98 should match the SERPS benefit forgone for women below age 46, and for men below age 53.

PERSONAL PENSIONS

Your **earnings** is another factor in making the decision to contract-out. If you are likely to be a low earner – earning less than £11,000 a year as at mid-1996 – for the most of your foreseeable future, you would be better off staying in SERPS, because it at least gives you a safety net. But if you expect to live the major part of your working life in the fast lane, with its attendant job-hopping, to back up your optimism you should seriously consider *contracting-out*. If you do this you should really top up your *personal pension* contributions above the basic *rebate-only* level.

Your **health** also has to be taken into consideration. If you are not too fit, remember that in England and Wales, SERPS will not be payable to your unmarried partner on your premature death. But if you have an *Appropriate personal pension* you can leave your pension fund to them if you die before drawing your pension.

Warning: It really is important to accept that it is highly improbable that just using your National Insurance rebate money to fund a *personal pension* will be enough to provide you with a decent pension, however young you are when you start. It is therefore important to add new money to it, preferably from the outset, by making regular monthly contributions. You should also consider increasing these contributions as you get older and earn more money.

The SERPS pension itself is gradually being phased out and is expected to lose a lot of its buying power. This makes it more worthwhile considering setting out on your own. However, to some extent it is a gamble: you might have been better off staying in SERPS, but then on the other hand you might not. Your decision to leave SERPS depends on whether you think your favoured insurance company will offer you a better return on your money in the long term than the state.

Using the SERPS rebate to contract-out has some long-term conditions which may not suit you. Some of the state pension rights which you have given up to 'go private' must be protected under a rule called *Protected rights*. *Protected rights* conditions are:

- You cannot take the *Protected rights* part of your pension until you reach age 60, which applies to both men and women. If you have made additional contributions you can draw a pension based on that part of your fund at any time after age 50, but not from the contracted-out (protected rights) part. This means, for example, that if your total contributions are double the rebate, you will be able to draw half your fund at 50 and convert that into an *annuity*, but you will have to leave the other half until you reach the state pension age. Of course, the remainder of the fund will continue to be invested and – hopefully – keep growing.

- You cannot draw a **lump sum** from the SERPS rebate part of your pension fund though you can do this from a straightforward *personal pension* or a company *money purchase* pension scheme. However, you can draw a lump sum from the part of the pension fund built up with any extra money you contribute. This means that if your total contributions are double the rebate you have received, you can draw a lump sum of 25% of half the fund, ie. 12.5% of the total.

- Once you start drawing your *personal pension*, the protected rights part must be increased by a minimum of 3% a year, or in line with the Retail Price Index if lower. On your death, a continuing pension – of 50% – must be provided for your

spouse (if you have one) provided he or she is aged 45 or more, or has a dependent child.
- *Protected rights* offer you no protection if your contracted-out pension turns out to be worse than SERPS would have been. The Government will not make up the difference.

The decision to contract-out of SERPS must be made before 5 April in any one year, as the system only deals in **full** tax years. The rebates will be reviewed every five years and the Government will indicate the new levels for the following five years. This should make it easier to plan ahead.

If you do decide to contract-out then you must place all of each year's rebate in a single plan. However, if you are not in the company scheme, there is nothing to stop you setting up another personal pension for other contributions. In fact, you can have as many *personal pensions* as you like (provided that your contributions to them fall within the Inland Revenue limits). You can contribute to as many as you like – but it wouldn't normally be sensible because of the management charges you have to pay on each plan. That being said, if you make large contributions, there is still a case in favour of having more than one. It enables you to spread your investments a bit more.

Your employer can contribute to personal pensions

If you are employed, but there is no company scheme, and you decide to take out a *personal pension* – whether a SERPS rebate plan or a fully fledged *personal pension* – you can ask your employer to contribute to it. But he may prefer not to contribute to your *personal pension*. You can't insist that he does.

Portability

Portability is one of the marvellous advantages of *personal pensions*. It is a great plus for people who expect to change their jobs a few times in their career, for example those working in publishing, marketing, the leisure industry and the construction industry. *Personal pensions* really come into their own for women who are far more likely to change jobs because of enforced career breaks, perhaps to bring up the children or look after sick relations.

Company *final salary* schemes should carry wealth warnings for job-hoppers. People who change jobs tend to put in too little time with each firm to build up a decent pension and leave a trail of pension rights behind which will be less than if they had stayed with one employer. See **Table 10** (page 82), which illustrates the effect of moving jobs on final salary company pensions.

If you work for companies with *money purchase* schemes, then you should get some protection as the money that has built up is earmarked for you personally, and your share of the fund should keep growing after you leave. However, you cannot be sure that all your employers will have *money purchase* schemes.

It is sometimes possible to draw your money out of a previous employers' pension scheme and put it into a buy-out bond or a *personal pension* of your own. However, if in future, or if you are starting out on your career, you might do better to settle for a *personal pension* if you expect to make a few job changes over the years. You can continue to invest in your *personal pension* regardless of who employs you – or if you become self-employed.

Retirement at 50

You will have to wait until you reach the statutory retirement age (currently 65 for men and 60 for women) before you can draw any state pensions, but you can start drawing the new-style *personal pensions* at any time from age 50 (or even earlier if you're in serious ill health). But if you have a *contracted-out* plan then you cannot draw that portion which is based on your SERPS contributions. If you have an old style *Retirement Annuity Plan* you cannot start drawing it until you are 60 although you can transfer it to a *personal pension* plan in return for a potentially reduced lump-sum option. Also, you could start drawing on it if you are in serious ill health.

Many people wish to retire from their main career in their fifties. They sometimes want to try a new career or set up their own business. By the time you are in your fifties you should have a clear idea of whether you will have sufficient pension on which to live comfortably. If you wish to take another job, and therefore have an income from another source, you may decide not to draw your pension, or only draw part of it. Just knowing you have enough reserves to retire on may well give you the confidence to try something new.

Many *personal pensions* are devised in such a way that they are split into 'clusters' of 10 (or more) policies, so that you can draw your pension in stages – usually 10. If you do this, you can draw off a tax-free lump sum of up to 25% from each policy at the same time you start drawing the pension from it, if you wish. But you cannot take the cash and defer the pension. By adopting this strategy, the rest of your fund has the chance to grow, giving you an even bigger potential pension for later. You can even continue contributing to it, provided that you are still earning.

If you are seriously incapacitated, you can sometimes start drawing your *personal pension* before you are 50. You will have to ask your pension provider for details. Also, if you belong to a special category of employment (see **Table 17**, below), you may be allowed to draw your *personal pension* early. The table shows whom the Inland Revenue allows to retire early and start drawing their *personal pension*, or *Retirement Annuity Plan*:

Table 17: Minimum retirement ages for special occupations

Profession or occupation	Retirement age
Airline pilots	55*
Athletes (appearance and prize money only)	35
Badminton players	35
Boxers	35
Brass instrumentalists	55*
Circus animal trainers	50
Cricketers	40
Croupiers	50*
Cyclists (professional)	35
Dancers	35
Distant water trawlermen	55*
Divers (saturation, deep sea and free swimming)	40
Firemen (part-time)	55*
Footballers	35
Golfers (tournament earnings)	40
Inshore fishermen	55*
Jockeys – flat racing	45
– national hunt	35
Martial art instructors	50*
Models	35

Moneybroker dealers (excluding directors and managers responsible for dealers)	50*
Moneybroker dealers (directors and managers responsible for dealers)	55*
Motorcycle riders (motocross or road racing)	40
Motor racing drivers	40
Newscasters (ITV)	50*
Nurses, physiotherapists, midwives or health visitors who are females	55*
Offshore riggers	50*
Psychiatrists (who are also maximum part-time specialists employed in the NHS solely in the treatment of the mentally disordered)	55*
Royal Marine Reservists (non-commissioned)	45
Rugby League players	35
Rugby League referees	50*
Singers	55*
Skiers (downhill)	30
Speedway riders	40
Squash players	35
Table tennis players	35
Tennis players (including Real Tennis)	35
Territorial Army members	50
Trapeze artists	40
Wrestlers	35

* People with old-style Retirement Annuity Plans can retire at 50 if they transfer to a new-style personal pension. (See next page: Old-style versus new-style personal pensions.)

Lump sum

If you have a new-style *personal pension*, you can draw a tax-free lump sum of 25% of the fund, excluding any *Protected rights* portion which was financed by your SERPS rebate. If you take a lump sum, then you reduce the amount of money you can turn into an income. But you can reinvest the cash elsewhere to increase your income.

Those of you with an old style *Retirement Annuity Plan* have to follow different rules. These rules say that generally the maximum lump sum you can draw is three times the remaining pension, after the cash has been withdrawn. This figure is difficult to quantify because it is tied to prevailing *annuity* rates at the time you make the decision. However, it usually works out at more than 25% of the fund (therefore it is a bigger lump sum than is available to *personal pension* holders). The older you are when you take up this option the larger the lump sum is, and men get more than women of the same age.

Another rule says that if you started contributing to *Retirement Annuity Plans* on or after 17 March 1987, the maximum lump sum you can draw from **each** plan is £150,000. As you can have a maximum of 10 such plans – in the unlikely event that you have built up vast sums in each, totalling **£4.5m** – then you could draw a total lump sum of **£1.5m**. People with *personal pensions* suffer no such limitations – they can draw 25% regardless of how much is left.

Old-style versus new-style personal pensions

This brings us to a comparison between old-style *Retirement Annuity Plans* and the new-style *personal pensions*. If you have an old-style plan is it worth your while converting it, usually for a minimal administrative charge, into a new-style pension?

PERSONAL PENSIONS

- If you want to retire, or start drawing your pension before you are 60, then you will need to convert your policy to a new-style plan. But you needn't do it now: wait until you want to retire.

- If your main priority is to be able to draw the largest tax-free lump sum, then you would normally be better off staying put and holding on to your *Retirement Annuity Plan*. If you have a **pre-March 1987** *Retirement Annuity Plan* and you intend to work after normal retirement age, then it will increasingly pay you to stay put. However, if you have a **post-March 1987** retirement *annuity*, and if your fund is likely to be in excess of £600,000, then you should consider conversion, unless you have set up the 10-arrangement plan set out above.

    You also have to take into account that, with a *Retirement Annuity Plan*, you can only buy your *annuity* from the company you have been investing with. You **do not have** an *open market option*. This could lock you into a poor *annuity* provider – UNLESS you convert to a *personal pension* plan, which is easily done, at relatively short notice. Therefore, at retirement, you have to balance the advantage of the larger lump sum against the need for a better *annuity*. It will, of course, depend on the situation at the time.

- If you are employed, but not in a company contracted-out pension, then you can use a *personal pension* plan to contract-out personally and get the SERPS rebate. You cannot use an old-style plan to contract-out.

- If you are a higher earner and have an old-style retirement *annuity* pension, your contributions will not be restricted by the *earnings cap* considerations. If you convert it to a new *personal pension* contract, they will.

Pin-money pensions

If you have a money-making sideline and are in a company pension scheme, then you are normally allowed to contribute to a *personal pension* based on your freelance earnings. This will give you added flexibility at retirement.

Life cover

A major disadvantage of a *personal pension* for employees who choose not to join the company pension scheme is that they often lose out on life cover. Many companies offer life assurance and sickness benefits and widow/ers' benefits for their employees – only if they are in the company pension scheme. This type of benefit is very valuable because it could:

- Pay up to two-thirds of your salary to you if you are so seriously incapacitated because of an accident (at work, or in your own time) or through ill health that you are unable to work.
- Pay out a lump sum of up to four years' salary to your dependants if you die while still working for the firm.
- Pay out a spouse's pension of up to two-thirds of your current earnings if you die while still working for your employer.

However, you can fill in some of the gaps by including tax-free **life cover** under your *personal pension*. Whatever type of *personal pension* you have, you are allowed to get full tax relief at your highest rate of tax on life assurance premiums of up to 5% of your normal earnings (often called net relevant earnings). This 5% comes out of the Inland Revenue limits on contributions to *personal pensions* for your age. You can have life cover to leave your dependants with a lump sum as long as you hold the plan. It may be a good idea to write it in *trust*.

If you want some protection in the case of being incapacitated and unable to work, then you should consider paying for a waiver of premium benefit. This may cost an extra 5% or so of your contribution, but it means that if you are unable to work you stop contributing to your pension and the insurance contributes instead, so that your pension doesn't suffer.

Self-administered personal pension schemes

It is possible for you to set up your own self-administered *personal pension* scheme, in which you select your own investments, rather than rely on the traditional with-profits or unit-linked investments that form the basis of most *personal pensions*. They could be really exciting and challenging to administer, but this is a highly specialised area.

They require Inland Revenue approval before you can go ahead, and once they are set up the Inland Revenue tends to monitor them closely. Also, you will almost certainly need the advice of a very experienced financial adviser who specialises in such schemes to ensure that you conform to the rules and, more importantly, that the money will be there when you want to retire.

These schemes are not to be recommended to anyone who hasn't got the right professional expertise, or the money to buy the quality of advice that is necessary, to prevent the scheme ending in disaster and/or perpetual correspondence with the Inland Revenue.

Chapter 5:
How to choose a personal pension

Now we get to two of the most dangerous areas. First of all you have to find one of the best companies from whom to buy your *personal pension,* and then when you retire you have to find the right company from whom to buy your *annuity.*

There is a major difference between:

- **investing** your pension contributions with one of the best pension providers; and
- turning that into **revenue** (pension) when you retire.

These problems lead to the following questions:

- How do you choose a *personal pension*? There are hundreds of financial organisations out there trying to get your business. They include insurance companies, friendly societies, unit trust companies, financial management companies, banks and building societies.

- What do you do with the money you have painstakingly built up? You don't have to buy your pension *annuity* from the same company: indeed it is often better not to!

In choosing the best *personal pension* for you, you can ask your favourite insurance company or, preferably, your independent financial adviser (IFA), to help you narrow the field – or you can do your own research.

In this chapter we explain how to choose a financial adviser, but first of all we will look at the varieties of pension plan you can buy.

When you start looking for a *personal pension* plan you will find a bewildering range of choice and lots of people only too keen to advise you. It pays to remember that there is no such animal as the **best** *personal pension* plan for everyone. There is a great deal of competition for *personal pension* business and companies are always trying to improve their contracts to keep ahead of the competition. They usually do this by offering greater flexibility.

The art of pension planning is to find a contract that offers **you** exactly what you **want** and **need**. The following 15 point checklist should help you make your decisions. We will go through each point in turn, explaining its relevance.

- The need for good investment performance.

- Types of plan (with-profits versus unit-linked) and assessment of past investment performance.

- Choosing between with-profits and unit-linked.

- Can you switch between funds easily and cheaply?

- Can you switch/redirect future contributions to a different

type of pension without penalty, if you become ineligible to have a *personal pension*?
- Can you stop, start and vary your contributions easily and without penalty?
- Can automatic increases be built into contributions?
- Can you have a waiver of contributions if you become too ill to work?
- Can you easily arrange a loan against the fund if you hit a financial crisis?
- Can you retire early without penalty?
- Can you have an *open market option* without penalty?
- Can you phase in your pension over a number of years?
- Is life cover available within the plan?
- If you die before retirement will your dependants get all your fund returned to them?
- Is the plan easy to read?

Need for good investment performance

The most important requirement for a pension fund is that it grows sufficiently well to provide you with a healthy fund with which to buy a super *annuity* when you retire. The same rule applies to all pensions. While, as all financial advisers will tell you to the point of tedium, 'past performance is no guarantee of future performance', financial advisers themselves always look at past performance of pension funds before making any recommendations. But they concentrate on consistency. They rely heavily on the regular statistics published in such journals as the insurance industry bible, *Money Management*. It is published by the *Financial Times* group and is readily available to consumers from all major newsagents.

Obviously, the size of your pension depends partly on how much you contribute, so it is not worth short-changing yourself. As a very rough guideline, we suggest that by investing 10% of your earnings for most of your working life you should produce a satisfactory pension. If you discover in your mid-forties or by your fifties that your fund is not growing fast enough, then you can consider taking advantage of the increased maximum contributions for older people in order to increase your contributions.

It is very important to take professional advice or to do some DIY research, since the difference between the best and the worst performing companies is enormous. The worst performing company could leave you with a pension fund worth barely half the value of the best.

Money Management carries out *personal pensions* surveys from time to time, to establish the best performing policies. The latest one before publication of this book was in the March 1996 issue, which related to data collated as at 1 December 1995 (see **Table 18**, page 132).

Types of plan

With-profits

While you can buy pension plans from a number of sources, with-profits plans are only managed by life assurance companies and friendly societies. With-profits pension plans are a version of the familiar old endowment policies with which you might be financing the purchase of your house. Basically, your contributions are added to other people's contributions in the company's with-profits fund and invested in a broad range of investments. This may include shares (equities), Government stocks, property and money markets.

The ultimate value of your pension will depend on the company's investment performance and the attitude of the company's *actuary*, a very up-market walking calculator-cum-economist-cum-statistician. Each year the *actuary* works out how much profit has been made on the total fund's investments. He (and it usually is a he) adds the income received on the investments to the increase in their value over the past year and allocates a share of this increase to each of the with-profits shareholders. He will not allocate all the money. Some is held back for the company's reserves and to pay benefits at a later date. When the *actuary* has decided on the allocation, he will declare an annual *bonus*. The company will add this sum to your pension fund. Once this is done, the *bonus* can never be deducted and future bonuses will be calculated on the increased value of the fund.

As well as annual bonuses, there are special so-called terminal bonuses which are added when you finally use your fund to buy your *annuity*, or which are added to your policy to pay to your heirs if you die before you can draw your pension.

Unit-linked

There are special unit-linked funds (a variety of unit trusts) which are authorised to be used for pension plans. There is no tax on any income (such as from dividends) or profits they make. You can buy them from insurance companies, friendly societies, unit trust companies and certain banks and building societies.

In unit-linked pension plans you do not get the same cushioning effect you get with with-profits plans (which lock in some of your gains every year) because your contributions, less management charges, are used to buy units in your chosen fund(s). The value of your total fund when you retire depends on the value of your units at that time. This means that if the stockmarket is doing badly on the day you want to cash in your fund to buy your pension *annuity*, then the value of your fund will be depressed. This is because the price of your units varies from day to day and thereby changes the value of your fund. If the prices are down, then the money available to buy your pension will be reduced.

You may be able to wait for conditions to improve, and delay the time at which you start drawing your pension; on the other hand, of course, the stockmarket may be very buoyant and it may be an excellent time to sell.

Companies which provide unit-linked pension plans usually offer a wide selection of funds from which to choose. This may be a mixed blessing, depending on the type of funds you select. You might be unlucky and choose the wrong funds at the wrong time, when they are expensive, and find that they are not performing very well when you retire. However, one advantage with unit-linked plans is that you can switch your investments from one fund to another within the same company. Typically, you get one free switch a year but may have to pay a fee for any others.

Funds are usually arranged in sectors. For example you can choose to invest all or some of your money in United Kingdom equities (shares in UK companies), in European companies, in Pacific companies, in a broad range of international shares, or in property. All these sectors carry varying degrees of risk, ie.

the risk that your money might fall in value. However, all unit-linked pension fund managers offer at least one straightforward *managed* or *general* fund which is designed to be less risky. This type of fund might not build up as fast as some others, but over the distance they have a good track record.

Some offer funds invested in absolutely safe Government stocks, but if you select these too early in your pension planning career you will be sacrificing potential growth. However, it could well make sense, as you near retirement age, to switch the bulk of your unit-linked pension funds into such safe havens.

Unitised with-profits

Unitised with-profit funds are a sort of half-way house between with-profits and unit-linked plans. You buy units in a with-profits fund so that the value of your fund cannot fall and every year you are allocated a *bonus* depending on the performance of the fund. The *bonus* increases the value of your units and you should qualify for a terminal *bonus* when you retire. Only insurance companies and friendly societies are allowed to offer unitised with-profits pension plans, though you can buy them through banks and building societies, some of whom now own insurance companies.

Unitised with-profits funds were only introduced in the mid-1980s, so their track record is too short to provide a sound basis for assessment.

Deposit-based plans

Deposit-based or deposit administration plans are basically 'high' interest deposit accounts offered by some insurance companies, building societies and banks. They offer a higher rate of interest than normal deposit accounts and the interest earned is tax free, regardless of whether you are a standard or higher-rate taxpayer. The income from this interest is reinvested and so the fund builds up faster than if you had left the cash in a normal deposit account. They are risk-free because the value of your capital cannot fall. However, in the long term, they are unlikely to give you as good a result as more risky forms of pension plan.

The main use for this type of plan is to protect the value of your pension fund in the last two or three years before you expect to retire. If, for example, you have a unit-linked pension fund and have made some good gains, you can transfer all or some of your money into one of these cash-type funds. Some pension companies do it automatically if you ask them. This manoeuvre protects your profits while still adding some interest. Usually you will find that when the stockmarket is depressed interest rates tend to rise and, conversely, when the stockmarket is buoyant interest rates tend to decrease.

With-profits versus unit-linked

It has become fashionable to persuade investors to buy unit-linked plans instead of the traditional with-profits plans. There are two schools of thought about this. With-profits are considered more prudent because once the annual bonuses (also called reversionary bonuses) have been allocated to you they cannot be taken away. Unit-linked plans are considered more risky as there are few or no guarantees of their value at retirement.

The school that prefers with-profits plans points out some very good and consistent results from the leading life assurance companies – saying that while unit-linked funds may, and sometimes do, outperform the best with-profits plans, there are more, consistently reliable with-profits plans than unit-linked plans. Also, that the odds of picking the right unit-linked plan are stacked against you.

Anyone whose unit-linked plan matured just **after** the UK stockmarket crash in 1987 would agree. On the other hand, if their unit-linked plan matured just **before** the crash they would disagree.

The undecided school suggests that you could compromise between the two and select a unitised with-profits fund, or at least put some of your money into such a fund, and the rest elsewhere. Alternatively, you could divide your contributions between a full-blooded with-profits plan and a more exciting unit-linked fund.

This leaves the *deposit-based* schemes. In the short term they are considered very good for holding the value of your money and perhaps increasing your capital a little above the rate of inflation. However, they are not advised for anyone bar the very timid or those within about five years of retirement who sensibly wish to lock in their gains and 'insure' against a stockmarket crash. The long-term growth potential of deposit-based funds is poor.

THE COMPLETE GUIDE TO PERSONAL PENSIONS

Table 18: Selection from the *Money Management personal pensions* survey, with-profits policies, March 1996

It shows the variations in pension fund performances, over 20 years, and how much you would have been entitled to if you had invested £200 a month for the periods listed. Best results in bold

	Monthly premium of £200			
Years	5	10	15	20
	£	£	£	£
Axa Equity & Law	14,414	48,483	134,145	**330,938**
Britannia Life	13,266	40,855	96,263	210,674
Clerical Medical	13,709	47,065	114,462	—
Commercial Union	12,708	44,835	113,835	**308,399**
Co-op Insurance	**15,223**	**52,266**	126,200	281,919
Eagle Star	13,304	46,383	121,530	—
Equitable Life	**15,068**	44,174	126,785	295,080
Friends Provident	14,263	**49,250**	**138,710**	—
GA Life	**14,400**	45,468	124,620	—
Legal & General	14,073	46,607	121,930	283,506
NFU Mutual	**14,713**	42,186	115,092	259,169
NPI	13,417	41,056	107,655	270,395
National Mutual	13,626	45,954	123,721	281,365
Norwich Union	13,878	44,353	**141,446**	**302,511**
Pearl Assurance	**14,367**	46,099	**138,608**	**346,395**
Royal Insurance	13,782	37,742	96,247	245,675
Royal London	**14,366**	**47,782**	127,124	—
Scottish Amicable	14,101	**50,276**	118,832	275,977
Scottish Equitable	14,229	40,708	125,424	269,003
Scottish Friendly	**15,282**	**48,798**	124,768	—
Scottish Life	13,354	42,811	124,747	295,580

Scottish Mutual	13,362	46,521	**133,929**	293,944
Scottish Provident	14,214	45,688	122,592	278,255
Scottish Widows	13,832	41,143	122,109	297,550
Standard Life	13,891	37,571	116,682	292,535
Sun Alliance	13,691	39,082	107,693	246,679
Sun Life	14,162	**48,393**	**131,954**	**319,003**
Wesleyan Ass'nce	**14,407**	**47,496**	128,086	342,317
Highest fund	15,282	52,266	141,446	346,395
Average fund	13,971	44,529	122,328	287,413
Lowest fund	12,708	36,156	96,247	210,674

Table courtesy of Money Management.

Flexibility

In the lifetime of a personal pension, which may be anything up to 45 years, many things can happen on the world stage that might influence your approach to investing. Eastern Europe may take off, so might China, or exciting new developments might occur in the energy sector. Therefore, you should consider at the outset what flexibility is built into your choice. Even if you choose a with-profits plan you can arrange a transfer to another plan, such as a *Freestanding AVC* (additional voluntary contribution), an executive *personal pension*, or even another company, without penalty if you become ineligible to have a *personal pension*. You should ask the company when you take out the plan whether they will penalise you for doing this; some companies will not. If you buy a unit-linked plan it is important to check that you have the facility to switch between the various funds at a reasonable cost. Some charge you for this, others allow one or two free switches a year.

Can you stop, start and vary your contributions easily and without penalty? Before you take out a pension plan you should decide how often you wish to make contributions – monthly, annually or occasionally, or any combination of the three. If you have regular income you will probably prefer to pay monthly, with the option of topping up occasionally. For example, towards the end of the tax year you may wish to use up more of your tax-free allowance, but not want to be committed to doing this every year. If your employers are contributing they would almost certainly prefer you to have a monthly contract. If you are self-employed you will probably prefer a flexible arrangement so you can base your decision on each year's profit.

At some stage in your life you may want to stop your contributions for a while: you might get a job which offers an absolutely super pension scheme; or you may stop working altogether for a while because of redundancy or illness; or, if you are self-employed you may go through a rough patch. Women have to take into account the prospect of career breaks to bring up children or to look after ailing relations. It is therefore sensible to make sure that you can stop, start or vary your contributions easily and without penalty.

If you choose monthly premiums, check the minimum number of payments required. Different companies have different rules, but most will insist that you pay the contributions for at least one year, while some have minimum monthly payment levels. If you want to select a with-profits plan, you need to ensure that if you do take a break from contributions for a while, your fund will continue to grow and attract bonuses until you restart your contributions or want to draw your pension.

Can automatic increases be built into contributions? A sensible arrangement, if you are making regular contributions, is to build in some increases as you earn more money. Quite a number of companies now ask if you wish your contributions to increase automatically each year by a certain percentage such as the Retail Price Index or the Average Earnings Index (which is higher). This saves you from the trouble of having to write to them every time you have a pay rise to ask them to increase your contributions. It also helps to ensure that your fund will increase in step with your increased earnings.

Can you have a waiver of contributions if you become too ill to work? One potentially valuable option, which may cost an extra 5% or so on your premiums, is waiver of contributions. This means that if you become too ill to work for any reason (excluding conditions such as alcoholism or drug addiction) the company will keep up your contributions at the level they were immediately prior to your illness. If you have built-in automatic contributions the pension provider will possibly increase their contributions at the higher rate. They will pay this money until you return to work, or even up to your normal retirement date if you are never physically able to return to work. This protects your pension arrangements for your normal working lifetime, and you can draw your pension at the age you originally agreed.

Can you easily arrange a loan against the fund if you hit a financial crisis? Some people are wary about contributing as much as they would wish to their *personal pension* because they cannot touch the money until they retire. Therefore, some companies will allow you the facility of borrowing against your fund in cases of emergency so that you do not feel that you have kissed the money goodbye until retirement. The rules restrict you to a certain percentage of the fund. In practice, very few people actually take out such loans, but they can be useful in a crisis. On the other hand, it is always possible to go to a bank or building society and take out an interest-only loan which would be payable at retirement using the tax-free cash from the pension. In the majority of cases you might be better off doing this.

Can you retire early without penalty? A surprising number of plans penalise you for bringing forward the date at which you wish to retire. They do this because they pay out more commission to the pensions salesperson on longer-term contracts than on shorter-term contracts, and they want their money back. They also like to know exactly how long they are going to have your money in order to plan their investment strategy.

Unless you are very close to retiring it is probably difficult to know what the exact date will be. There may be all sorts of reasons why you want to bring the date forward: illness, redundancy, or just because you feel like it. Besides, if you are in a unit-linked contract and the stockmarket is doing incredibly well, you might want to pull out when you think your fund is close to peaking, without having to worry about the pension provider charging you. Therefore, if you have a choice of two similar plans that you like, and one penalises you for retiring early and the other doesn't, you would be best advised to take the one that doesn't. While some companies don't penalise you at all, some impose penalties of up to some 14% of the size of the fund. The table overleaf reveals what penalties (if any) companies impose on with-profits *personal pension* policyholders who retire early.

Table 19: Surrender penalties – What you get if you retire early – with-profit plans

Policyholders pay a monthly premium of £200

Projected open market option funds for male aged 40 at outset

	To selected retirement date		Initial term 25 years but taking early retirement after	
	20 years £	15 years £	20 years £	15 years £
Some of the best – those who penalise you the least, if at all				
Clerical Medical	113,435	65,492	113,001	64,614
Commercial Union	107,802	63,133	107,802	62,684
Equitable Life	115,922	67,651	115,922	67,651
GA Life	109,850	63,878	109,850	62,865
NPI	111,061	65,253	111,061	65,253
Some of the worst – those who penalise you the most				
AXA Equity & Law	104,907	63,428	97,662	55,907
Friends Provident	107,997	63,150	93,659	54,073
Scottish Equitable	110,703	63,984	100,668	59,234
Scottish Life	113,484	66,949	108,769	62,538
Sun Life	106,870	62,192	104,972	55,474

Source: *Money Management, Early Retirement Survey, January 1996.*

There is an alternative: if you really like a certain plan, and the only flaw you can find is that it penalises you for early retirement, all you have to do to keep your options open is to say that you want to retire at 50 (the earliest permissible age). You can then retire whenever you want to after that date and it will make absolutely no difference to your position. Neither you nor your fund will be damaged by this move. Besides, you will probably have to pay less commission because salesmen's commission is usually enhanced by longer-term policies. However, like all the good things in life, there is a catch: if you are unable to work through sickness or injury and you have paid for a waiver of premium, the insurance company will cease to waive at age 50! You win some and you lose some.

Can you phase in your pension over a number of years? Being able to do that, which means that you can start drawing your pension in stages, could be quite useful. This facility, which is also known as a 'multiple plan facility', means that the contract is arranged into a cluster of, say, 10 policies. At its simplest, you can start drawing your pension in up to 10 stages, or any suitable number of combinations. For example you may like to draw 7/10ths to start with and then add the other 3/10ths one at a time over three years. Each time you do this, your lump sum is adjusted accordingly, so that you can draw off a lump sum of 25% of the fraction of the fund you have cashed in. It may be an option that you do not wish to take up, but experience shows that people who have retired appreciate the choice. The circumstances under which you may use the option include:

- If it is your only pension, and you cannot expect anything from your employers, you ought to have a very large pension fund. It is recommended that anything under £100,000 may make this an expensive option because of the costs of setting up a series of annuities.

- Retiring from your main job and taking a part-time job, but needing to top up your income while preserving part of your fund intact, with growth potential.

- Retiring with a small company pension if, for instance, you have been an early leaver and want to keep part of your *personal pension* fund intact for a while.
- You may want to build in an element of inflation-proofing and leave some of your fund still growing, even if you are not still contributing to it.
- Your spouse or partner may still be working when you retire and you do not need to draw your full fund.

Can you have an *open market* option **without penalty?** You must be allowed to use your fund to buy your *annuity* from whomsoever you choose. This facility could be quite important when you retire. The best company with which to build up your *personal pension* fund may not be the best one from which to buy your *annuity*. Specialising in fund building is one expertise, specialising in providing good annuities is another. However, some pension providers, who also offer annuities, charge you for taking your money away to buy an *annuity* elsewhere. They penalise you by offering you an *annuity* from their own range based on one value of the fund, and by offering a lower value of the fund if you take your money away. If they offer superb annuities this might not matter. But if they offer dreadful rates it could make a major difference – thousands of pounds – to your retirement income.

Even if you know, at the time you start your personal pension, that the pension provider has an excellent reputation for annuities as well as fund building, you should still ensure that you won't be penalised for taking up your *open market option* later, because requirement may be many years away, and the company may not provide such good annuities by then, or other people may offer superior ones that suit your needs better.

Is life cover available with the plan? Some insurance companies offer you the option of taking out life cover as part of your pension plan. The premiums are eligible for tax relief. You can take this option provided the maximum you pay is 5% of your normal earnings and that, when added to your pension contributions, it does not exceed the maximum contribution the Inland Revenue allows. This can be a very cheap way of getting term assurance to protect your dependants. It is a useful if you don't qualify for the life cover that people in company pension schemes often receive automatically.

If you die before retirement will your dependants get all your fund returned to them? Most pension providers will pay the total of your fund to your nominated dependants if you die before drawing it – but some don't! There are four typical arrangements:

– Return of fund (ROF) is usually the best deal for the investors, as your estate gets a full return of fund which will be valued at the date of death (including any bonuses to which you may be due).

The following mainly apply to the old *Retirement Annuity Plans*:

– Return of contributions with interest (RWI) is next in the pecking order. This means that your estate gets the sum total of all your premiums with compound interest at a rate which should be stated in the plan literature. All growth in the fund is ignored. The only time when this would be the best buy would be if there had been a prolonged stock-market recession and the value of shares had sunk.

- Return with no interest (RNI) is much less favourable because your contributions are returned without taking account of fund growth, and without any interest. This means that your heirs only get your contributions back, which is a pretty poor deal unless the pension fund provider offers some really super extra concessions like very favourable *annuity* rates if you survive to draw your pension.

- No return of funds (NR) is the worst possible deal. As its name suggests your estate will receive nothing if you die before you start drawing your pension. Go into this type of contract with your eyes wide open and read the small print very carefully. Make sure the benefits outweigh the disadvantages – such as highly preferential *annuity* rates if you survive.

If you have death benefits under your plan, it would be sensible to write them in trust, unless it is to be assigned to cover a loan, such as a pensions mortgage. The benefits then fall outside your estate and will not be liable for Inheritance Tax.

Is the plan easy to read? Beware of the glossy pension plan brochure that is complicated. If it is difficult to read you might miss some important details and find that what you thought you had bought and what you actually bought are quite different. Most pension providers now make the effort to be clear and include a question and answer section. There is nothing wrong with this, but they might not answer **your** questions. If you have any questions, or if there is anything you do not understand, do not hesitate to ask the company or your financial adviser to explain it – **in writing.**

Financial strength of the company

Last, but by no means least, you ought to give some consideration to the quality of the company you are considering. When you select a company you want to be sure that it is well run and can produce consistently high investment performance. You want to know that it has sufficient reserves to absorb dramas such as the international stockmarkets taking a nosedive. This is especially important if you have a with-profits policy because you don't want to miss any annual *bonus*, and you want a good terminal *bonus* when you cash in your fund. If you choose a unit-linked pension plan you have to bear in mind that the fund managers cannot use any reserves to help you out.

The normal investor will have difficulty establishing the financial strength of a company. You can discover this by reading the trade press such as *Money Management*. It regularly reports on the best performing *personal pension* schemes and the strongest pensions companies. But as this is a bit like hard work for the average pensions investor, the best solution probably is to ask a professional financial adviser.

How to choose a financial adviser

Having decided that you wish to go ahead and buy a *personal pension* and the main ingredients that you want it to have, you now have some more decisions to make. Which plan do you want and who are you going to buy it from? You have the choice of:

- Going direct to a company (or, preferably, more than one) that you have discovered from the league tables published in the financial pages of the national newspapers (or, better still, the trade press, such as *Money Management*) has a

HOW TO CHOOSE A PERSONAL PENSION

very good investment track record. In this case you will deal with a company representative.

- Going to an authorised independent financial adviser (IFA) – or more than one – and asking them to recommend a good plan that fulfils your requirements. They can recommend from all the companies in the market.

- Going to a financial adviser who is tied to a particular insurance company. They will have an in-depth knowledge of the products available from their company.

- Going to your bank manager or building society manager and asking them to recommend a pension plan. As many banks and building societies are 'tied', which means that they have arranged to sell only one company's plans, it is often much the same as going direct to an insurance or unit trust company.

- Going to your accountant or solicitor. If they advise on personal finance they will be independent and free to recommend from all the companies in the market.

Warning: You must make sure that the financial adviser is a registered member of the Personal Investment Authority (PIA) and fully authorised and qualified to advise you. You can ring the PIA's Central Register (a computerised information database) direct on 0171 929 3652 to check whether the IFA is authorised. You can also ring Independent Financial Advisers Promotion (IFAP) on their helpline, 0117 971 1177, or write to them at 17-19 Emery Road, Brislington, Bristol BS4 5PF, and they will give you a list of three authorised independent financial advisers in your area.

If you would rather pay a fee for the advice than let the adviser accept commission – which comes out of your payments – you could ring the *Money Management* hotline, on 01179 769 444, and they will give you the names of six fee-based independent financial advisers in your area. They will also send you a leaflet explaining the pros and cons of fee-paying as opposed to commission-paying advice.

The meeting

Once you have decided who to go to for financial advice, you need to do some preparation to define your requirements. Run the ruler over your finances so you know where you stand. Before you go to the meeting you need to establish your financial situation.

If you have all the details at your fingertips during the meeting you will be able to concentrate on the answers to your questions rather than worrying about where you left your insurance policy documents. If you appear confident and organised you will get the best from the meeting.

The sort of questions your adviser will need to ask are listed in the following checklist:

- how much you have invested, and where it is;

- your financial commitments such as mortgage, loans, private education for the children, or responsibility for dependants; your current income and likely income;

- any life insurance (premiums and sums assured) or pension arrangements you already have, from previous company pension schemes;

- how much you think you can afford to contribute to your pension;

- your tax position, and your tax number;
- your National Insurance number and a note of any missing years for events such as career breaks;
- your proposed retirement age;
- your investment philosophy, eg. cautious, realistic or adventurous;
- your state of health.

Pension planning is quite complex, and you may need several meetings with the adviser of your choice before you come to any firm decisions. Don't be in too much of a hurry. Remember, since your pension benefits may well benefit other members of your family, it pays to discuss your arrangements thoroughly with those likely to be affected and to review your overall life assurance and health cover, plus any need for inheritance tax planning.

Chapter 6:
Using PEPs to pep up your pension

We have covered the major planks of conventional pension planning – state pensions, company pensions and *personal pensions* – and now come to the increasingly popular *Personal Equity Plans*. They were launched in 1987 by Nigel Lawson, the then Chancellor of the Exchequer, and have become so popular that by the end of the 1994/95 tax year investors had piled more than £22 billion into them.

PEPs are a special type of tax-efficient unit trust (or investment trust), and should normally only be considered as an extension to pension planning rather than a replacement for normal pensions. They are only suitable for people who are **financially disciplined** – because PEPs are easily and totally accessible, and if you are susceptible to raiding the piggy-bank you could wreck your long-term retirement planning.

They are also suitable for people who have surplus income and who cannot put in enough time in their company pension scheme to qualify for a decent pension, and for people who have already taken up their maximum contribution options, and want to top up their retirement funds.

It must be made clear that there is an element of risk because few PEPs come with any form of guarantee, but many have a long enough track record for you or your financial adviser to identify a pretty reliable one. They should be considered as a medium-term investment, therefore more suitable for people who have **at least five years** to go before retirement, or before they expect to cash them in.

Tax

One of the main differences between pensions and PEPs, apart from the potential to build up an accessible retirement nest-egg, is in the tax treatment of the two savings vehicles.

With pension income, you get tax relief **before** you retire: you get tax relief on your **contributions** to your pension (whether company pension or *personal pension*) but any income arising from that, whether through the company scheme or annuities, is liable to income tax. Basically that means that, excluding any special tax allowances you may qualify for, **any** income you draw over £3,765 from a pension is liable for tax (1996/97). The figure rises to £5,555 for people who qualify for the married couple's allowance.

For people aged 65, the single person's allowance, before they become liable for tax on their pension income, increases to £4,910 a year, and for married couples it increases to £8,025. But remember that any income you draw from state pensions is included in the calculations. The basic state pension is currently (1996/97) £3,180 a year, with an additional £1,903 for a wife

USING PEPS TO PEP UP YOUR PENSION

who does not qualify for a pension in her own right. So you can see that unless you take a defensive position, quite a chunk of your retirement income is going to disappear in tax.

If, however, you use *PEPs* as part of your retirement planning, you effectively get tax relief **after** you retire. You usually pay for PEPs out of income that has already been taxed. So if you draw off income from your PEPs it is not liable for income tax, and when you cash them in you are not liable for capital gains tax either. You don't get taxed twice. Also, there is no income tax on dividends from shares held in PEPs, and no capital gains tax. Hence they build up faster than conventional unit trusts or investment trusts.

Therefore, if your retirement income is likely to exceed the £3,765 a year threshold, and especially if you are likely to be a higher-rate (40%) taxpayer in retirement, there is a good case for considering buying PEPs as part of your pension planning.

Ground rules

PEP investors must be aged 18 or more and be resident in the UK for tax purposes, but not necessarily be a taxpayer. The PEP must be managed by a PEP plan manager approved by the Inland Revenue.

You may invest up to £6,000 a year in a general PEP. (Unlike *personal pensions*, you cannot carry forward any unused allowance.) You can also invest up to £3,000 a year in a single-company PEP, as well as, or instead of, a general PEP. You can only select one plan manager each tax year for a general PEP, but you may be able to spread your investment across a number of funds offered by that PEP manager.

General PEPs account for the lion's share of the market and

come in a wide variety of forms. What they have in common is that they accept up to £6,000 a year from each investor, paid as a lump sum or in monthly instalments, for investment in company shares directly, or in pooled funds such as unit trusts and investment trusts.

Single-company PEPs, on the other hand, have an annual investment limit of £3,000 and, as the name implies, the money is used to buy shares in just one particular company. If you already have shares in a good company you can arrange to put them in a single-company PEP, subject to the £3,000 a year rule. It will cost you something because technically you have to sell them and buy them back, but many single-company PEP managers offer special deals to keep the price of buying and selling down. There is no requirement for a general PEP and a company PEP bought in the same tax year to be managed by the same investment group.

The overall investment limit of £9,000 applies to each individual over 18, so a husband and wife can invest up to £18,000 between them each year. But you cannot buy PEPs in joint names. An existing PEP from a previous tax year may be transferred to a new scheme without affecting the current year's allowances.

Within this framework, there are two other categories of PEP – qualifying and non-qualifying. Up to £6,000 may be invested in *qualifying* funds in which at least 50% of the underlying assets is invested in the UK or other EU countries. Within that £6,000 allowance you may invest up to £1,500 in a non-qualifying fund, which can invest more than 50% of the money in non-UK or non-EU countries. This would include, for instance, International Funds or those specialising in the Pacific area or the United States. If you use the £1,500 non-qualifying allowance, you may still top up your PEP (with the same manager) up to the maximum £6,000.

One last ground rule, which has implications for people using PEPs for retirement planning:

– On the death of a PEP investor, the tax-free status of the PEP ceases. The capital accrued will remain tax-exempt, but future capital gains and dividends become liable for tax from the date of death. A PEP, therefore, may not be passed to a surviving spouse or to another beneficiary on death. Beneficiaries will have to cash in any PEPs or accept that they have reverted to normal unit trusts (or investment trusts) and may be liable for tax on future gains and income.

Choosing a PEP

With some 1,200 *Personal Equity Plans* out there, how do you choose one? You can either go the DIY route, which could be risky, or you can take advice. But in either case, you first need to decide how **risk-adverse** you are. This will influence your final choice. Some PEPs are more volatile than others, even if over the distance they do well, and if you think you may need to draw your money out at short notice, you want to be reasonably confident that your PEP will not be not suffering from a temporary blip – or worse – on the Stock Exchange.

Even if you totally trust your independent financial adviser to give you appropriate advice **for you,** you would be well advised to do some easy homework. Reading the national press personal finance pages on a Saturday is a good start, to get the feel of the subject. They are always publishing helpful articles about PEPs, and their pages are full of advertisements for PEPs, especially in the spring before the end of the tax year.

By law, advertisements for PEPs must stress that a good fund track record is no guarantee of how well the fund will perform in future. However, anyone who ignores a good consistent track record and relies on gut reaction, fashion or sticking a pin in a page, is taking unnecessary risks. A good consistent fund, measured over at least five years, is often a better bet than one which hits the top of some performance league table at the end of six months or a year.

But don't rush your fences. Just because the newspapers appear to be concentrating on one particular area or fund doesn't mean that it is right for you. Some PEPs suffer from being fashionable for a while, and then fading into the background – if not oblivion. Therefore it is worth the time sitting back and observing for a while.

You can't realistically expect to pick a PEP that is always No. 1 in its sector from one year to five: as with choosing a *personal pension* plan, the best you can hope to achieve is to pick a PEP that is usually up with the big boys.

PEP specialist independent financial advisers Chase de Vere recommend that before choosing a PEP, you should draw up a shortlist of requirements to help you whittle down the types of PEP you should consider.

For a start, while general PEPs can accept up to £6,000 each year, many people do not have such a large sum of capital available; many managers accept monthly contributions of up to £500, but the minimum monthly contribution can be as low as £10. Some investors like to combine the two approaches, perhaps by investing £2,400 at the outset, and following that up with £300 a month for the rest of the year.

Some PEP managers have restrictions of their own, so it is worth keeping your mind open: be prepared for one or two disappointments. For example, you might really fancy one PEP that appears to suit your investment criteria only to discover that the managers will not accept monthly contributions.

Types of PEP

It is useful to understand the difference between the various types of PEP, such as unit trust PEPs and investment trust PEPs, which are often regarded as variations on the same theme because they have common characteristics. They are both collective investment vehicles, substantially investing in shares listed on the Stock Exchange.

Unit trust PEPs are simpler to understand: you buy units in the trust at the 'offer' price and sell them later at the 'bid' price, typically 5%-6% less. The difference in the 'bid-offer spread', as they call it, is the initial management charge, out of which may come commission to the financial adviser. But investment trusts, in which you are technically a shareholder in a company that trades in shares only, operate differently. The difference is too technical to go into here, but over the distance they tend to give you a bigger return.

Then there are Corporate Bond PEPs. These tend to pay particularly high levels of income and are generally less volatile than shares. They spread your investments over shares, bonds and convertible shares. There is still an element of risk, but could be useful for people wishing to increase their income – at the expense of some growth, of course.

Performance

The fortunes of PEPs fluctuate more or less in line with the Stock Exchange, and not every year is a good year. But you should take a long-term view of them – generally accepted as a minimum of five years. Unlike some shares, they certainly won't leap up in price overnight. However, over the distance you should normally be able to rely on your investments growing faster than leaving your money invested in a building society account.

No one can predict how much your PEP will grow. Some years are better than others. For example 1995 was a good year for PEP investors, but you can't expect the same performance this year, or next, or any other year. In 1995, fully qualifying unit trust PEPs grew at an average 19.2% over the year, and fully qualifying investment trust PEPs averaged 14.7%, according to Chase de Vere. It lists the following average performance figures, to the end of 1995.

Table 20: Average PEP results to end 1995

£1,000 invested over	3 years	5 years	7 years
Average qualifying unit trust PEP	£1,526.59	£2,058.79	£2,234.78
Average qualifying investment trust PEP	£1,575.43	£2,158.64	£2,550.53
Halifax 90 day Solid Gold Account	£1,138.46	£1,358.46	£1,740.96

Source: Chase de Vere, PEPGuide.

Table 21: Top 20 qualifying unit trusts: £1,000 invested over 5 years

Company	Trust	5 years
1 Hill Samuel	UK Emerging Companies	£3,579.87
2 Morgan Grenfell	Europe Growth	£3,349.95
3 Jupiter	Income	£3,291.72
4 Edinburgh	UK Smaller Companies	£3,025.61
5 Thornton	UK Smaller Companies	£2,953.04
6 Pembroke	Growth	£2,925.53
7 Morgan Grenfell	Europa	£2,919.09
8 Schroder	UK Enterprise	£2,833.70
9 Jupiter	UK Growth	£2,793.63
10 Smith & Williamson	Smaller Securities	£2,780.56
11 Credit Suisse	Smaller Companies	£2,770.13
12 HTR	UK Smaller Companies	£2,703.48
13 Perpetual	High Income	£2,700.70
14 Britannia	Smaller Companies	£2,637.32
15 Credit Suisse	High Income Portfolio	£2,635.60
16 St James	UK & General Progressive	£2,631.40
17 Perpetual	UK Growth	£2,617.25
18 Royal Life	UK Emerging Companies	£2,595.63
19 Lazard	UK Smaller Companies Growth	£2,590.33
20 Henry Cook Arkwright	Growth	£2,572.52

Source: Chase de Vere PEPGuide, January 1996.

Access

As already explained, access to your investment is a serious consideration. You should regard PEPs as being a medium-term investment. If you believe that you can't afford to leave the money alone for five years or more, you have to accept the risk of selling your PEP at a time when it is worth less than the money you paid for it. However, you can always draw some money by cashing in some or all the units, without jeopardising your tax position. There may be 'exit charges' involved if the PEP hasn't been invested for a minimum period set by the managers – probably two or three years.

Income

In retirement, or even before, you may wish to start increasing your income. This is easily done. You can change any of your existing PEPs any time you like, to increase your income, rather than keep growing your money pile. You can either do this by:

- cashing in some or all of your units in one or all of your PEPs, from time to time – tax free, of course; or by
- transferring your growth PEP(s) to an income PEP, which could give you an income.

While most PEP funds are designed to increase your capital, some specialise in using your investment to give you an income without having to cash in your units. There are some PEPs that are exceptionally good at providing an income, from the dividends of the companies they invest your money in, while still keeping your capital intact – and growing. But, as at 1996, don't expect the earth from the income: 3% to 5% is pretty good even compared with building society rates (as at May 1996) but it is tax free, and your capital has the potential to keep growing. If you invested £6,000 in an income PEP now, that would give you a return of about £180 – £300 a year.

But, if you had invested £6,000 in a growth PEP five years ago and it was now worth a – feasible – £12,000, your tax-free income could be £360 to £600, subject to prevailing circumstances.

An alternative scenario is to plan to draw the capital, ie. cash in your total holding in each PEP in stages, cashing in the first one first, in Year 8, and the second one in Year 9, and so on. Say that you invest £3,000 a year in a good growth PEP for each of the next eight years, then (to be cautious) let us assume they each double in value after that eight years. At the end of each year from the end of Year 8, you could draw up to £6,000, tax free.

Just think what would happen if you were able to start investing a minimum of £3,000 a year for every year from the age of 40 to 65: barring accidents, you could have very significant funds at retirement.

For this chapter we are indebted to help from: Chase de Vere Investments, independent financial advisers who specialise in PEPs. They publish an easy to read **PEPGuide** for potential investors. It costs about £12.95, and you can get an updated performance chart two or three times a year for £2 each. They are available from: Chase de Vere Investments, 63 Lincoln's Inn Fields, London WC2A 3BR.

Chapter 7:
Making the best of your pension

Choosing a retirement date, and choosing an annuity

There is more to getting the best out of your pension than just swapping your pay cheque for a pension cheque. For a start, if you have a *personal pension* you do not necessarily take all the money at once. You might prefer to draw your money in stages, thereby building in some inflation-proofing. Or, if you are going to have some other income, you might not wish to draw your pension for a while. Drawing a pension early will decrease its value and drawing it later should enhance your income.

Questions you need to answer:

– Do you want to retire early?
– Do you want to retire at the statutory retirement age?

- Do you want to retire late?
- Should you take part of your pension as a lump sum (*commute* it)?
- Should you use the fund to take an income for life?
- If you have a *personal pension*, or *money purchase* plan, what sort of *annuity* should you get?
- Do you want to increase your income or your capital?

Early retirement

Retiring early has become very fashionable. If you have been careful with your money, have a good pension behind you, or have received a nice inheritance, you may wish to do so. On the other hand, you might want to leave your main career behind and set up a small business of your own, secure in the knowledge that you have your pension to fall back on.

Before making the decision to retire early you ought to have a pensions audit (see Chapter 1) to make sure that you can afford it. For instance, the mortgage is usually one of the worst expenses; will it be paid off or are your repayments so small that they hardly come into the equation? Will your retirement income be enough to live on happily or will you have to scratch around to make ends meet?

State pensions

As far as your state pensions are concerned, you will not normally be able to draw either the basic pension or SERPS until you reach the statutory pensionable age, currently 60 for women and 65 for men, although women's retirement age is gradually being put back. All women who were born before 6 April 1950 can draw their state pension at 60. This will gradually change so that women born after 5 March 1955 will have to wait until they are 65.

Also, you ought to bear in mind that unless you continue to pay *National Insurance contributions* at the voluntary rate of £5.95 a week (1996/97), your basic state pension might be reduced when you draw it. To keep their basic state pension intact women normally have to contribute to National Insurance for about 39 years, and men for 44 years.

Your pension will be scaled down if you pay for fewer years. Broadly, you lose £1 a week for every year that you don't make any contributions (unless you've been exempted). The table below illustrates how this works:

Table 22: Basic state pension: How much you can expect if you do not keep up voluntary National Insurance payments on early retirement (1996/97 figures).

Qualifying years*	Men %	Men £	Women %	Women £
44	100	61.15	100	61.15
43	98	59.92	100	61.15
42	96	58.70	100	61.15
41	94	57.48	100	61.15
40	91	55.64	100	61.15
39	89	54.42	98	59.92
38	87	53.20	95	58.10
37	85	51.97	93	56.86
36	82	50.14	90	55.03
35	80	48.92	88	53.81

* A qualifying year means every full year you have paid the full National Insurance contributions, including years when you were 'excused payment' because you were sick, redundant, or had Home Responsibility Protection for bringing up children or looking after sick relatives.

Company pensions

Most company pension schemes have traditionally set the standard retirement age at 60 for women and 65 for men, but this is now changing; they are now gradually equalising company retirement ages in line with the new state rules, and ultimately both men and women may have to retire at the same age. This is usually 65, but many employers have equalised at other ages. However, subject to the company pension scheme rules, the Inland Revenue will still allow men to draw their company pension from age 50 and women from age 45, or 10 years before the company's normal retirement age, whichever is the later. But beware: company pension schemes tend to penalise you if you retire early.

Final salary

If you are in a *final salary* scheme you may qualify for a 1/60th pension for every year's service, but you don't usually get that if you retire early. Therefore, by retiring early, you not only lose the opportunity to build up a bigger pension, but also the value of your ultimate pension is likely to be reduced for every such year. This could be very painful. If you wish to retire early you should check the company handbook to see whether it will adversely affect your pension, and by how much.

You should also check what will happen to your pension if you **delay** drawing it until some time after you have left the company. You can only delay drawing the pension until the normal retirement date of the company. As from 1 January 1991, if you leave the company the worst they can do is to peg your pension at the date you left and then annually add on 5% or a figure equal to the annual increases in the Retail Price Index (whichever is the lower). The company must then pay the increased figure.

The company is allowed to increase your pension by a larger figure, even **fully** inflation-proof it – if it operates a generous scheme. Different rules will apply if the company scheme is *contracted-out* of the *State Earnings Related Pension Scheme*.

Obviously, if you opt to defer your pension in this way, you will need to make sure that you have enough to live on in the meantime. However, if you retire early on grounds of ill health, you may find you do not suffer financially as well. You may be allowed to get the full pension you have qualified for so far. Much depends on the attitude of your pension scheme trustees who may credit you with the pension you would have earned if you had been able to work to normal retirement age. For example, if you had been in the 1/60th pension scheme for 20 years and would normally expect to put in another 10 years before retirement, the trustees may agree to give you a pension which assumes that you had completed 30 years' service – ie. 30/60ths or half-pay.

Money purchase

If you are contributing to the firm's *money purchase* pension, you should find out the size of your fund before going ahead with your retirement plans. You should ask the personnel department for details and you could also ask them how much income the fund would generate at current interest rates. Basically, they will arrange to buy you the type of *annuity* you want (see Annuities, page 172). Beware, if the scheme is contracted-out, you can't take that part of the benefit until you reach 60.

Personal pensions

If you have a new-style *personal pension* you can start drawing it at any time after age 50. If you have an old-style *personal pension* (a Section 226 *Retirement Annuity Plan*) you will not be able to start drawing it until you reach age 60, but it may be worth converting it to a new-style *personal pension*. Likewise, if you have a Section 32 *Buy-out plan,* you may not be able to start drawing from it before the retirement age set by the company pension scheme the money came from. However, you can convert it to a new-style *personal pension*. It is worth checking how much the insurance company you bought it from will charge you for doing this.

You could have another problem with *buy-out plans* if the company scheme you left was contracted-out of SERPS. Embedded in the plan will be something called the *Guaranteed Minimum Pension* (GMP). This is the part of the pension that was bought with your National Insurance contribution rebate to the company. You can take the benefits before state pensionable age, as long as the pension paid is at least equal to the *Guaranteed Minimum Pension.*

The rules are different for *Appropriate personal pensions* (APPs) for which you pay entirely or partly with your *National*

Insurance contributions. The rules changed as from 6 April 1996, when the Government relaxed them.

If your appropriate *personal pension* is **entirely** paid for out of the SERPS rebate then you will not be able to cash it in for an *annuity* until state retirement age. But you can start drawing off an income from age 60, and defer buying your *annuity* until normal retirement age, leaving your fund to build up. The sum you are allowed to withdraw is similar to that which your fund would provide as an *annuity*. You do not have to withdraw the maximum each year, but a minimum equal to 35% of the maximum. You can then leave the bulk of your fund to continue building up until state retirement age when you can buy your *annuity* with the remainder.

This facility will help men who wish to retire early, or start drawing their pension before the normal state retirement age of 65. It will also allow your spouse to draw the money if you die before age 60, or while withdrawing the money. There is no lower age limit for income withdrawal for a surviving spouse. If, however, there is no surviving spouse, the fund will pass to the estate of the deceased, subject to the appropriate tax, unless you have arranged to write your estate in trust and can pass the money to your nominated heirs.

But, if your *personal pension* is only partly paid for out of your SERPS rebate, and you have been making additional contributions, then you can draw the part of your fund that is not paid for out of the SERPS rebate. Alternatively, as from age 60 you can start drawing income while leaving the bulk of your fund to continue growing. But there is no guarantee that the money withdrawn from the fund will be replaced by investment growth from the remaining fund. Therefore, you should take financial advice if you wish to take the income withdrawal option.

Full details of the facility are included in a leaflet, 'Income withdrawal from your appropriate *personal pension*', No. PP6, which is available from the DSS by contacting the DSS Pensions Info-Line on 0345 31 32 33. The line is open 24 hours a day and calls are charged at local rates. Alternatively, the leaflet can be obtained by post from: DSS Pensions, FREEPOST BS5555/1, Bristol BS99 1BL.

Whichever type of *personal pension* you have, if you wish to consider retiring early, you should check how much money is in your fund and the prices of annuities that your pension provider offers. At the same time you should either find out for yourself, or ask your financial adviser to find, the best rates on the open market. The best pension fund investment companies do not necessarily offer the best *annuity* rates (see Annuities, page 172).

For everyone with *personal pension* or *Retirement Annuity Plans*, timing the cashing in of your fund can be quite critical. If your fund is unit-linked and the stockmarket is performing badly, then it might be a good idea to delay drawing your pension, or only drawing part of it. Conversely, because the income you can get from annuities is influenced by prevailing interest rates, and because interest rates tend to be higher when the stockmarket is down, you might get a better income at this stage. It is all a matter of judgement and your individual requirements.

Retiring at normal age

If you retire with a company pension at the normal age, your main consideration is probably whether you should take part of your pension as a tax-free sum (See 'Should you take a lump sum', page 170). If you work for a company with a final salary scheme, your decision is final and cannot be changed. This means that once you start drawing your pension you will receive that level of income, plus any inflation-proofing built- in, until you die.

However, if you wish to retire at the normal age with a *personal pension* (old-style or new-style) you might like to consider the merits of drawing your pension in stages. The advantage of doing this is that you have the chance of boosting your retirement income later. For instance, if you draw half or two-thirds of your pension fund at the beginning of your retirement, then you can leave the rest of your fund to build up until you need to increase your retirement income. By then your fund should have grown and you can start drawing the remaining part of your pension as you wish.

The ability to draw your pension in stages can be useful, too, if you intend to carry on working part-time, or if your spouse or partner is able to bring in enough money to pay some of the bills meantime. The longer you leave your pension, the greater its potential size.

Retiring late

Some people will be fortunate enough to actually enjoy their work and not want to be forced to retire just because they have reached retirement age. Some may be unlucky enough to need to carry on working because their pension planning started too late, or because they could not afford to save enough. However, there are some financial rewards for retiring late. For example, the delay increases both your basic state pension and SERPS by about 37.5% over the five years after retirement at normal age. As it is inflation-proofed as well, this could be worth waiting for.

The choices are fully explained in Chapter 2 (page 41), but it works like this: for every week you delay in taking your state pensions, each £1 of pension will be increased by 1/7th of a penny, provided that you do this for at least seven weeks during the five years, starting on the day you reached state pensionable age.

An easier figure to remember is that your pensions increase by about 7.5% each full year. At today's prices, with the full basic state pension at £61.15 a week (£3,179.80 a year), your pension will increase to about £65.73 if you defer it for one year; and it will increase to £84.08 a week (£4,372 a year) if you defer it for the full five years. In the case of a married couple, who currently qualify for £97.75 a week (£5,083 a year) between them, it would rise to £134.40 a week (£6,989 a year) after the full five years.

SERPS and the Graduated Pension (for what that's worth) will go up by the same percentage. You have to defer **all** your state pensions, you cannot defer just one of them. However, the state system is quite flexible. If you opt to defer your state pensions, you can change your mind at any time. It makes sense to choose the end of a seven-week period, counting from the day you reached state pensionable age, as payments will not be made for part of seven weeks. Also, once you have started drawing the state pension, you can stop at any time within five years and start building up an increased pension for later. However, you can only change your mind once. You cannot get any more increases after you are 65 (women) or 70 (men).

Do remember to tell the Department of Social Security of your plans. They should write to you four months before you reach the statutory retirement age 'inviting' you to claim your pension. Also, if you have started drawing your pension and want to stop, you need to inform them. Just stopping cashing in your pension cheque is not enough. You should complete Department of Social Security Form BR432 in DSS leaflet NI92, 'Giving up your retirement pension to earn extra'. It is available from your local DSS office.

If you do defer your state pension for the full five years you will need to live for another 13 years 6 months to break even and get the maximum benefit in terms of the money you have not drawn. This means that men will have to live until they are about 83 and women until they are 78 to benefit fully. These figures exceed the normal life expectancy of men, but not of women. Mortality figures show that on average women can expect to live until age 86, while men who retire at 65 can expect to live to age 81.

Just because you are not drawing your state pension does not mean that you cannot draw your *personal pension* or your company pension. On the other hand, you can draw your state pension and leave any others to build up. Alternatively, you can draw your state pensions and invest the money in a *personal pension* for future use – provided that you are still earning. In order to be allowed to pay **all** your full basic state pension of £61.15 a week (£3,179.80 a year) into a *personal pension*:

- a woman aged 60 will need to earn a minimum of £9,085 a year (or, if self-employed, she must make a taxable profit of that sum);
- a woman aged 61 or more, and a man aged 65, will need to earn a minimum of £7,950 a year.

Should you take a lump sum?

Should you take part of your pension as a lump sum (*commute* it)?

Most company pension schemes allow you to draw off a lump sum when you retire. You can usually do this by sacrificing some of your potential retirement income. Employees in the public sector usually automatically get a pension that is based on 80ths **plus** a lump sum and have no choice but to accept the lump sum. Most other people have to make the decision for themselves.

If you qualify for a full two-thirds pension, the maximum lump sum you can draw from a *final salary* scheme is one and a half times your final salary. Therefore if you are earning £20,000 when you retire, the absolute maximum lump sum you can draw is £30,000. However, employees who joined a pension after 14 March 1989 suffer an *earnings cap* which means that earnings over £82,200 (1996/97) don't count. So the maximum for high earners in this category is £123,300 even if they are earning £100,000 or more.

In practice very few people ever qualify for a full pension or full lump sum – indeed it is estimated that only 10% of the working population do. What usually happens is that the maximum lump sum you can draw is 3/80ths of *final salary* for every year you have been in the scheme, whether *final salary* or *money purchase*. So, if you have been in the firm's scheme for 20 years, the maximum lump sum you can get is 3/80ths *final salary* x 20, ie. 60/80ths or three-quarters of your pay.

For example, if you were a member of your company pension scheme before 17 March 1987, the maximum lump sum you can draw is illustrated in the table below:

Table 23: Maximum lump sum you can draw from a company pension scheme

Years of service	Maximum lump sum expressed as a fraction of final salary	Percentage of final salary
1-8	3/80ths for each year	3.75% for each year
9	30/80ths	37.50%
10	36/80ths	45.00%
11	42/80ths	52.50%
12	48/80ths	60.00%
13	54/80ths	67.50%
14	63/80ths	78.75%
15	72/80ths	90.00%
16	81/80ths	101.25%
17	90/80ths	112.50%
18	99/80ths	123.75%
19	108/80ths	135.00%
20 or more	120/80ths	150.00%

However, if you take the cash your pension income will suffer, unless, as already mentioned, you are in a public sector scheme. The amount by which it will be reduced depends on your age and sex, but in broad terms (excepting people in public sector pension schemes, who, as already mentioned, get a lump sum anyway), you can expect your pension to be reduced by about £1 for each £10 of cash you take.

The actual reduction is on a straightforward sliding scale of between 8.19% for women aged 55 and 10.2% for women aged 65; 9.8% for men aged 60, and 12.8% for men aged 70. Therefore the longer you wait to draw your pension the less it is reduced for the same amount of lump sum. The same tax-free limits also apply to *money purchase* company schemes.

Usually, the maximum you can take as a lump sum if you are in a *personal pension* scheme is 25% of the fund. However, if the scheme has contracted-out of SERPS, the part of the fund that was paid for with the National Insurance rebate cannot be swapped or used when working out the size of the fund for this purpose. But *personal pensions* set up **before** July 1989 **can** include that *Protected rights* portion when calculating 25% of the fund.

Whether you opt for a lump sum or not depends mainly on whether you want to maximise your income, which is, after all, what pensions are all about. Purists argue that you should take all the fund as income because it is deferred pay. However, the income you get from your pension is liable to tax, therefore you might be better off drawing the lump sum and buying a *purchased life annuity* with it to supplement your main pension. It is a more tax-efficient vehicle. Likewise, if you have a *personal pension* you might prefer to buy a *level annuity* with 75% of the fund and a *purchased life annuity* with the 25% lump sum you draw off. You need to take professional advice at the time when you know what the respective *annuity* rates are for both types of *annuity*.

Annuities

If you have a *personal pension*, a *Retirement Annuity Plan*, or a *company money purchase plan*, you will eventually need to use most of the fund to buy an *annuity* which will provide you with an income for the rest of your life.

Picking a good pension fund is a piece of cake compared with the complications of choosing an *annuity*. Very little is published about them and yet they are one of the most crucial financial planning decisions you can make. You can lose thousands of pounds a year in income by making the wrong decision, so it is important to make the right one. You don't get a second chance.

A pension *annuity* provides an income for life. It is bought with your pension fund from the cash available after taking out any lump sum you wish to draw. You have **no option** but to buy a pension *annuity*, which is why it is also called a *compulsory purchase annuity* (CPA), with your pension fund, apart from any lump sum you draw. The Government has allowed you handsome tax relief on your contributions to encourage you to be independent in your retirement and to avoid your being a burden on the state, so they will not allow you to renege on that contract once you retire.

In a way, buying an *annuity* is rather like investing a lump sum in a high-interest building society account – the main difference being that you cannot get your capital back once you have invested it. However, in exchange, you should get a better guaranteed return for your money than you would by investing it for income anywhere else. You are guaranteed an income for life regardless of how long you live – whether for 10 years or 50. It is this guarantee that sets it apart.

When you are approaching retirement, your pension

provider should contact you with important information about the options available to you for maximising your income in retirement. They'll tell you exactly how much money you've accumulated in your pension plan over the years, and how most of this must normally be used to buy an *annuity*. They will also tell you how much you can draw off the fund as a tax-free lump sum.

The basics

Suppose you bought a simple level 10% *annuity* with the whole of your pension fund of £100,000: the insurance company will pay you £10,000 a year for the rest of your life. Basically, that means you get your money back in 10 years – but they have to carry on paying you £10,000 a year for as long as you live, regardless of what happens to *annuity* rates. If you draw off a lump sum of 25%, £25,000, you will only have £75,000 to buy the *annuity*, and at 10% that will pay you £7,500 a year for life.

People tend to buy their *annuity* from the insurance company with which they have built up their pension fund. **BUT** the best company with whom to build up your pension fund is rarely the best *annuity* provider.

Buying your annuity from your pension provider can be a terribly expensive mistake.

Not all pension providers offer annuities, but in any case you have what is called an *open market option* to buy your *annuity* from any authorised insurance company. The company that holds your funds may penalise you for taking the money away from them, but that can be a small price to pay for an improved *annuity* elsewhere.

Just as banks and building societies compete for customers with savings accounts that offer different rates of return, so life assurance companies offer different *annuity* rates. But these rates vary much more than ordinary interest rates. According to the *Annuity* Bureau, leading *annuity* advisers:

'The difference between the top companies and the bottom companies, incredibly, averages around 9% but can be as much as 25%.'

That's a lot of money. For an investment of £60,000 it can make the difference between having an income of £6,000 a year or £7,500. By buying from the wrong company you could be sacrificing £15,000 over 10 years. See the table below:

Table 24: The cost of choosing the wrong annuity supplier

Assumes you pay £60,000 for your annuity

	Pension paid to you now	Total income you WOULD receive After 10 yrs	After 15 yrs	After 20 yrs
Supplier A	£6,000pa	£60,000	£90,000	£120,000
Supplier B	£7,500pa	£75,000	£112,500	£150,000
Your extra income from Supplier B	**£1,500pa**	**£15,000**	**£22,500**	**£30,000**

Source: Annuity Bureau, Tel: 0171 620 4090.

So, unless you do some research, you could end up with a lower pension for the rest of your life. It really does pay to shop around and to ask firms like the *Annuity* Bureau or your independent financial adviser, who may already deal with them, to find the best deal for you. In a way it is like shopping around for the best building society high-interest account, but **more important because it is a once and for all decision.** You can't change your mind later.

It is important to bear in mind that the type of pension plan (or plans) you hold will dictate the amount of freedom you have in choosing your *annuity* benefits. Most individual *personal pensions* or *money purchase* schemes give complete freedom of choice, but if you (or your company scheme) have contracted out of the *State Earnings Related Pension Scheme (SERPS)*, a minimum level of benefits is compulsory.

If you have more than one type of pension plan (company schemes, transfer pensions, top-up plans, etc.), the benefits from each may or may not be compatible enough for you to amalgamate them and purchase just one *annuity*. Generally speaking, though, adding funds together will help you to secure the best rate of income.

Types of annuity

There are various types of *annuity*, each offering a different rate of return. The rates vary according to factors such as:

- your age when you take it out;
- your sex;
- whether you want to be paid monthly in advance or arrears, quarterly or annually;

- whether you want guarantee periods and, if so, for five years or 10 years;
- whether you want a level payment plan, or one which escalates in line with increases in the Retail Price Index;
- whether you want an *annuity* to be paid to your spouse if you die before he/she does;
- your state of health;
- whether you are a smoker/non-smoker.

Age

The older you are when you buy an *annuity*, the higher your income will be. Obviously the actuaries – the up-market statisticians who work out the figures – do not expect a 70-year-old to live as long as a 60-year-old, and therefore will be more generous to older people. Even a couple of years can make quite a significant difference in the payments.

Gender

Men get significantly bigger annuities than women of the same age because statistically they are expected to live for a shorter time. So the insurance company does not expect to have to pay men for as long as they expect to pay women. If you select a joint life *annuity*, which continues to pay out to your surviving spouse on your death, your spouse's age will have an added impact on the amount of your pension.

Payment intervals

Most people will expect to receive their pension cheque monthly, because it replaces their salary cheque, but if you are paid monthly in arrears, you can expect your income to increase a little. You can boost it further if it is paid quarterly in arrears. This is partly because the insurance company holds on to the money for longer and partly because there is reduced administration. You can expect the income from a pension paid monthly to be about 7% less than one paid annually. Choosing to be paid one month in advance could reduce your pension by 1%, and if you choose to be paid one year in advance it could reduce your pension by 15%.

Whether you make the decision to receive your cheque three months or one year in arrears will depend on your financial circumstances. For example, you may have been in a company pension for long enough to support your normal living expenses, and wish to use your AVCs or *personal pension* to pay for Christmas or holiday expenses.

Guarantee periods

Many people are worried about what will happen to their fund if they die shortly after starting to draw their pension. They think it is unfair to have spent umpteen years building up a good pension fund and then lose the bulk of it by dying prematurely. They want their families to get the benefit of the fund if they die early.

You can get round this by accepting a reduced pension and buying a *guaranteed annuity*. Most people want a five-year guarantee but some prefer a 10-year guarantee. This usually means that if you die within five years (or 10 years) of drawing your pension the company continues to pay the income to your estate until the agreed period has elapsed. Alternatively, if your selected guarantee period is no more than five years you could arrange for your dependants to be paid a lump sum, based on the unused proportion of your pension fund. Of course, if you select this guarantee option, the value of your *annuity* will be decreased. For example, a man aged 65 could expect 3% less income from a 5-year guarantee than from a pension with no guarantee at all. A 10-year guarantee would pay him about 8% less.

On the other hand, if your fund is large enough, over £100,000, you could consider phased retirement, in which you buy annuities in stages. This has the effect of keeping some of your capital intact, so that your heirs can inherit it if you die before you buy annuities with the remaining part of the fund (see Phased retirement, page 184).

Level payments or escalating payments

Annuities offering level payments are the simplest option. They are usually the most popular as initially you get the biggest possible pension, but their buying power will be eroded as inflation has its wicked way with your income. If inflation runs at an average of 5% a year the pension will lose a quarter of its value in about six years and halve in 14 years; whereas if inflation runs at 7.5% the pension will halve in 10 years, and reduce to one-third in 15 years.

Table 25: Effects of inflation on your pension

Buying power of £1,000 in the future

Inflation	5 years	10 years	15 years	20 years
2.5%	£884	£781	£690	£610
5.0%	£784	£614	£481	£377
7.5%	£697	£485	£338	£235
10.0%	£621	£386	£239	£149

If you are going to rely entirely on an *annuity* (plus your state pensions) for future income and expect to be drawing it for many years, then you could consider an *annuity* which pays out an increasing income. It will cost you, but may save you from financial embarrassment later if you live to a ripe old age. For example, opting for a 5% escalating *annuity* could reduce the first year's pension by around 42% for a 60-year-old man, by 36% for a 65-year-old man, and by 31% for a 70-year-old.

It is important to balance carefully what you need now against what you may need in future. Typically, a 60-year-old man would be aged about 81 before the value of an *annuity* escalating at 5% outweighed that of a non-escalating *annuity*. As the life expectancy of a 60-year-old man is another 21 years, there is no advantage. See table on the opposite page:

Table 26: Comparison of effect of 5% escalating annuity compared with a level annuity

Man aged 60, drawing £1,000 annuity

Age	Level	Escalating	Difference	Cumulative difference
60	£1,000	£ 580	-£420	-£ 420
61	£1,000	£ 609	-£391	-£ 811
62	£1,000	£ 639	-£361	-£1,172
63	£1,000	£ 671	-£329	-£1,501
64	£1,000	£ 705	-£295	-£1,796
65	£1,000	£ 740	-£260	-£2,056
66	£1,000	£ 777	-£223	-£2,279
67	£1,000	£ 816	-£184	-£2,463
68	£1,000	£ 856	-£144	-£2,607
69	£1,000	£ 899	-£101	-£2,708
70	£1,000	£944	-£56	-£2,764
71	£1,000	£992	-£8	-£2,772
72	£1,000	£1,041	+£41	-£2,731
73	£1,000	£1,093	+£93	-£2,638
74	£1,000	£1,148	+£148	-£2,490
75	£1,000	£1,205	+£205	-£2,285
76	£1,000	£1,266	+£266	-£2,019
77	£1,000	£1,329	+£329	-£1,690
78	£1,000	£1,395	+£395	-£1,295
79	£1,000	£1,465	+£465	-£830
80	£1,000	£1,538	+£538	-£292
81	£1,000	£1,615	+£615	+£323
82	£1,000	£1,696	+£696	+£1,019
83	£1,000	£1,781	+£781	+£1,800

You have the choice of levels of increase: normally 3%, 5% or 8.5% (the maximum) or Retail Price Index. Whichever level you choose you will then get a pension that rises at the rate you specified for the rest of your life. You may be able partially to inflation-proof your income by buying a with-profits plan or unit-linked plan. In a with-profits *annuity* you can expect annual bonuses which should increase your income over the distance. Unit-linked annuities are more risky and not for the timid. As unit-linked funds tend to be more volatile, the value of your fund can go down as well as up.

What happens is that your payments are calculated on the value of a pre-determined number of units. If the value of the units is low, then your income will reduce; likewise if the value of the units increases, then your pension will increase. This means your income will fluctuate, sometimes substantially, which is disconcerting and rarely appropriate for a pension.

Spouse's pension

Some people want to leave their spouse with a pension if they die before their spouse or partner. Again, at the expense of some current income, you can arrange for this facility. The amount by which the pension will be reduced will depend on the age and sex of your spouse. Therefore a man with a young wife will lose more than a woman with an older husband. Obviously the insurance company will not want to have to pay a 40-year-old widow a pension until she dies without charging significantly for this.

By choosing to leave your spouse with an *annuity* of 50% of yours, you can expect a reduction of 14% of the *annuity* you could get otherwise. However, most couples do opt for an *annuity* which will pay the spouse an income of between one-third and two-thirds of the basic level *annuity*.

State of health

Your state of health at the time you retire could have an influence on how much pension you can get from your *annuity*. Most *annuity* rates are based on the statistical evidence that men will live so long, and women so much longer. But if you are in really poor health when you retire and want to draw your pension there are special annuities, called 'impaired life' annuities, which offer specially high rates. If you are in this position you should take special financial advice before buying an *annuity*.

Smoker/non-smoker

Normally, companies don't make any distinction between smokers and non-smokers. When selling life policies insurance companies charge higher premiums for smokers, because they are widely thought to be damaging their health and therefore more likely to die early. However, they draw a line at offering better *annuity* rates to smokers on the understanding that they won't live so long, and therefore won't cost the insurance companies so much! Some insurers argue that to offer smokers better rates would mean condoning bad habits, and therefore they don't do it. However, one company – Stalwart Insurance – broke new ground in 1995 by making a speciality of offering smokers better rates. In their first few months these rates were consistently higher than most of their competitors.

Phased retirement

If your *personal pension* fund (or *Retirement Annuity Plan*) is big enough you could consider phased retirement. It is widely accepted that this is not worth considering unless you have a minimum of £100,000 in your fund.

Basically, this type of arrangement consists of a segmented pension, comprising up to 1,000 segments, of which you 'mature' only a sufficient number each year to provide you with your required income. The matured segments provide some tax-free cash, and you use the balance to purchase an *annuity* of your choice. Thus, the tax-free cash, coupled with the income from the *annuity*, will provide your required income for that year.

The same exercise is then repeated each subsequent year. The balance of the pension monies, which have not been matured, remain invested in the pension funds selected by you. These funds can be as risky or as secure as you wish, allowing the pension monies the opportunities for further growth.

Beware: This is a highly specialised area with inheritance tax planning advantages. It is essential that you take professional specialist advice.

Flexible pension

Alternatively, you could consider a flexible pension which allows you to delay your *annuity* purchase until age 75, while allowing you to take your tax-free cash and draw an income, within limits, from your *personal pension* fund which remains invested. This is especially valuable if you feel that *annuity* rates and/or your pension fund will increase during the deferral period, making the delay of your *annuity* purchase worthwhile. But, as this is a highly specialised area, it is essential that you take professional advice.

Under this type of arrangement, your family gets some protection. If you, the policyholder, die before age 75, then your surviving spouse or dependants have three options:

- Take a cash sum equal to the value of the remaining fund less income tax at 35%.
- Continue withdrawing income. An *annuity* must be purchased at what would have been the policyholder's 75th birthday, or the surviving spouse's 75th birthday, if earlier.
- Buy a conventional *annuity*.

Using your lump sum to boost income

If you decide (usually wisely) that your pension fund is to be spent exclusively on topping up your retirement income, then after you have spent the 75% or so, on your pension *annuity*, you still have 25% to spend. Rather than blowing it on a new car, holiday or whatever, you have any number of options.

Depending on how much money you get from your lump sum, you could be well advised to design yourself a **retirement portfolio.** The advantage of doing this is that it could help to spread the risk, and it gives you an added interest in following its progress.

Sensible options include the following straightforward investments:

- High-interest deposit accounts from banks and building societies.
- National Savings Income Bonds.
- *Tax Exempt Special Savings Accounts* (TESSAs) from building societies.

- Guaranteed Income Bonds (mainly from insurance companies).
- *Income Personal Equity Plans (PEPs).*
- Purchased life *annuities*.

Deposit accounts

'High' interest deposit accounts are mainly available from building societies and banks, but some insurance companies and unit trust companies are now moving into this area, and worth watching. Many of them offer you the facility to draw the interest monthly, or half yearly, rather than keep you waiting for the full year. If you draw the interest you keep your capital intact, but it will never have the opportunity to grow. However, if income is a priority, these accounts have the advantage of security and accessibility. The main disadvantage is that the spending power of your capital will decrease as inflation rises.

National Savings Pensioners Income Bonds

People aged 65 or more can buy National Savings Pensioners Income Bonds, the so-called Grannie Bonds, from the Post Office. They are absolutely safe, and especially valuable for pensioners who aren't likely to be liable for income tax. The interest is paid monthly, with no tax deducted. However, they also have their uses for pensioners who do pay tax, and who are prepared to sort out their tax payments at the end of the tax year.

Currently (May 1996) Pensioners Bonds pay an attractive 7% a year – which is fixed for five years. So, even if you have to pay tax at the standard rate of 24% you can get a tax-paid return of 5.32%, which is better than any building societies. The minimum investment is £500.

TESSAs

TESSAs, *Tax Exempt Special Savings Accounts*, mainly available from building societies, are designed as five-year savings plans, but you can draw tax-free income from them provided you stick to the rules. You can invest up to £3,000 in the first year (£6,000 for a husband and wife) in a TESSA and up to a total of £9,000 over five years. Some companies allow, indeed they encourage, you to invest the whole £9,000 with them at the start of the five years. They divert the 'excess' into another interest-bearing account and 'feed' the TESSA from this fund.

They were first introduced on 1 January 1991 and these early ones matured early in 1996. Investors who invested the full £9,000 at the start in one of the major building societies and banks for the full five years – **without drawing any interest** – ended up with anything from £12,209 – an increase of 35.6% (West Bromwich Building Society) to £11,492 – up 27.6% (Midland Bank). This is an average annual tax-free return of 8.83% to 7.04% respectively. Whether new investors will achieve such high returns is uncertain, because by early 1996 interest rates have tended to be much lower than they were during those five years. However, they are safe and sensible.

TESSAs are now much more complicated. You can buy equity-linked plans, and some which offer guarantees that you will make a minimum of something like 20% gross gain over the next five years – but that only averages 4% a year. Safe and sensible.

Some TESSAs still offer **income** rather than the prospect of growing your fund. But the returns are nowhere near as good. If income is your priority, it will pay to shop round, or ask your independent financial adviser to look up a decent TESSA for you.

Guaranteed Income Bonds

If you want short-term guaranteed income, you could consider Guaranteed Income Bonds (GIBs). They are offered from time to time by a number of companies. They guarantee a certain level of income for periods ranging from one to seven or more years. Normally, the longer the period the lower the interest. However, the income is fixed for the period, and you are offered a 'guarantee' that you will get your capital back at the end of the period.

Before committing yourself to a GIB, however, you must take a view on interest rates over the period you have selected. If you think they are likely to rise, you should be careful not to lock yourself into a long period at a low rate. Also remember that if inflation rises this will erode the real value of your income. Although interest rates have been dropping for a while and by Easter 1996 were at their lowest since the 1960s, a new Government with different economic policies could alter all this.

Also, remember that your guarantee of capital return is only as strong as the company you invest with, so make inquiries before you go ahead. You don't want your guarantee to be backed by the fund managers' big yachts and losing horses! Also, don't forget that once you invest your money you are locked in – no early withdrawals are allowed.

Income PEPs

As well as using *Personal Equity Plans* (PEPs) to supplement your pre-retirement fund-building, you can use them to supplement your retirement income. There are a number of Income PEPs which pay out a healthy regular – and tax-free – income, at the same time as having the potential to increase in value. They could be a good place for some of your lump sum.

Because a PEP is an equity-linked investment (ie. normally most of your money is invested in the stockmarket) its value can go down as well as up, so you should consult your financial adviser about suitable plans and decide on the level of risk you are prepared to accept. However, it could well be worth putting some of your lump sum into this type of investment. (For fuller details on PEPs, including Income PEPs, see Chapter 6.)

Purchased life annuities

The type of *annuity* you choose will depend on your financial circumstances, responsibilities to any dependants and your attitude to risk. But, while you must buy a pensions *annuity* with the bulk of your fund, you can gain some tax benefits buying a *purchased life annuity* with the lump sum. This may make sense if your main priority is to increase your income – which after all is what pensions are all about. You make gains by buying a purchased life *annuity* because the Inland Revenue accepts that part of your income is a return of capital – which is not taxable. It is tax efficient for basic-rate taxpayers, but especially beneficial for people who are likely to be higher-rate taxpayers after their retirement.

Using your lump sum for growth

If you wish to invest your tax-free lump for growth – to build up your nest-egg, for use at a later date – you should consider how accessible and safe you want your money to be. There are four categories of investment opportunity for you.

- **Savings on short call** such as instant access building society or bank deposit accounts. These accounts are partly intended to cushion you from emergencies such as the roof falling in, or a sudden family disaster where someone needs cash urgently, and partly to give you an instant source of cash in case an irresistible investment opportunity turns up.

- **Completely safe investments** which may offer a better rate of return than building societies. These include Guaranteed Growth Bonds.

- **Medium risk investments** such as 10-year with-profits endowment policies which lock in gains made each year, but where the return is uncertain since it is linked to stockmarket performance.

- **Higher risk investments** in carefully selected growth PEPs (see Chapter 6).

How you spread your lump sum between these various options is very much a matter of personal preference and need for security. It will depend on your attitude to risk in general, your view of the potential returns of an investment, and your financial circumstances. Overall, it would probably be wise to keep a sum equal to between three and six months' required income on short call and divide the rest between the others.

More exotic choices

If you fancy something more exotic, and are not risk adverse, you could try your hand punting in the stockmarket, but that is beyond the scope of this book. If you want to dabble in this area, the recommended easy-to-read book is Neil Stapley's *The Private Investor's Guide to the Stockmarket*, but remember the old saying: 'If you can't take a joke, don't join the stockmarket.'

GLOSSARY OF MAIN TERMS

Actuary
An expert who calculates the contributions needed to pay the pensions that have been promised. Actuaries are mathematicians, and their work involves using assumptions about probable life expectancy and investment returns for many years into the future. The Government *Actuary* is a senior civil servant, with a small department of his own, who does the forecasting for state and public sector pension schemes.

Added years
People in public sector pension schemes and in some private ones can make extra contributions to buy themselves extra years' pension in the scheme, within certain limits. This can prove a cost-effective way of providing extra pension for yourself.

Additional pension (1)
This is the earnings-related element of the state pension scheme known as the *State Earnings Related Pension Scheme* (SERPS), paid on top of the basic pension, which was introduced in 1978. The Department of Social Security works out the *additional pension* by taking your earnings between the Lower and Upper Earnings Levels,

currently – 1996/97 – between £61 and £455 a week, and recalculating them to take account of the increase in national average earnings between the date you earned the money and your retirement.

People who qualify for SERPS get an extra pension to add to their basic state pension. The Government is reducing the amount that will be available from SERPS, but this will not affect anyone in the state scheme retiring before the year 2000.

Additional pension (2)

Many married women are unable to qualify for a full basic state pension in their own right because they have had enforced career breaks, perhaps to bring up children or look after sick relations. Therefore, when their husband qualifies for the basic state pension, the wife is allowed an extra pension of her own, called an *additional pension*. Currently, 1996/97, where the husband may qualify for the full basic state pension of £3,180 a year, his wife should qualify for an *additional pension* of £1,903 a year.

Additional voluntary contributions (AVCs)

All occupational pension schemes must make arrangements for members to make *additional voluntary contributions*, which are usually referred to by their initials as AVCs. Due to the favourable tax position, this is a very good way of topping up your pension, though it is rather inflexible. Once the contributions are paid, they normally have to remain invested in the scheme until you reach the company's normal retirement age. You have to take the benefits at the same time that you draw your company pension.

Members of company pension schemes are also allowed to buy AVCs privately, when they are called *Freestanding* AVSs (FSAVCs). You can choose your own company from which to buy them.

GLOSSARY OF MAIN TERMS

Annuity
When people invest in *personal pensions, Retirement Annuity Plans*, or *money purchase pension schemes*, they build up their own 'pot' of money, a fund that must be used to buy an *annuity* when they wish to draw their pension. The provider, an authorised insurance company, agrees to pay you a regular sum throughout your lifetime. The amount is based on such factors as your age, your sex, and the rate on investment return the company expects to earn. (See also, *Open Market Options*.)

Appropriate Personal Pensions (APPs)
A type of *personal pension* into which you can transfer some of your *National Insurance contributions*, in order to contract-out of SERPS (the State Earnings Related Pension Scheme). COMPS (*Contracted-out Money Purchase Schemes*) are similar, and is the name for company schemes which are contracted out of SERPS.

Bonus
This is the sum added by an insurance company to the guaranteed sum in with-profits life and pensions policies, depending on how well their investments do. There are two main types: reversionary, or annual, bonuses which are declared each year and added to the policy at the end of the year; and terminal bonuses, which are added at the end of the policy term if the investment performance over the whole term of policy warrants it. Terminal bonuses are not guaranteed.

Buy-out plans
Also called Section 32 pensions, they are a type of *personal pension* into which you can transfer your pension benefits when you leave a company pension.

Carry-back
If you want to top up your *personal pension* (or *Retirement Annuity Plan*) above the annual level that the Inland Revenue allows you to, you are permitted to take up any unused tax relief for the previous six years.

Commutation (commute)
When you retire, you can turn part of your pension into a lump sum, which is tax free. This is called commuting it. *Personal pensions* usually allow you to draw 25% of the total fund and company schemes limit you to a sum which depends on the number of years you have been in the scheme. Roughly speaking, if you go for the maximum lump sum, you can expect to sacrifice £1 annual pension for every £10 to which you may be entitled. People in the public sector, such as civil servants, normally get a lump sum without having to *commute* their pensions.

COMPS
See *Appropriate Personal Pensions*

Contracting-out
If your employer's pension scheme gives a pension at least as good as the State Earnings Related Pension *(SERPS)*, the pension scheme is allowed to contract-out of *SERPS*. The employer uses the money to build up the company's pension fund. In return for this, both you and your employer pay lower *National Insurance contributions*. Individuals, not in a contracted-out company pension, can contract-out personally and have the National Insurance rebate invested.

Death in service benefits
Many companies will make special salary-related payments to

dependants of employees who die while still employed, and before retirement. They are often a mixture of lump sums and spouse's pensions.

Deferred annuity
Also called a deferred pension, this is an *annuity* which your employers can buy for you if you leave the company before retirement age. The *annuity* starts paying you when you retire.

Deposit-based schemes
Unlike most *personal pensions*, where your money is substantially invested in a mixture of equities (stocks and shares), with a *deposit-based scheme*, your money is invested in higher than usual interest deposit accounts with insurers, banks or building societies. They offer a higher rate of interest than normal savings accounts – because interest earned is tax free. They are effectively risk-free and useful when retirement is two or three years away, for protecting any gains you have made on equity-based investments.

Early leavers
Anyone who leaves a company pension scheme before being entitled to draw a pension is classified as an early leaver. This class of people could include people who have been members of the scheme for 20 or 30 years. Some employees can arrange to transfer their benefits, if appropriate, either to their new employer's scheme, or into a personal pension.

Earnings cap
Going hand in hand with the *pensions cap*, this is the upper limit to the earnings which are allowed to be taken into account when you contribute to *personal pensions*.

Final salary schemes

This is the main type of company pension scheme in the UK. The pension you are promised is related to your earnings at the time of retirement and the number of years that you have been in the scheme. Widely considered by employees to be the best pension scheme available, if you can put in enough time.

Freestanding AVCs, FSAVCs See *AVCs*

Group personal pensions

These are like normal *personal pensions*, offered by employers who don't have an occupational pension scheme for their staff. Because the company buys them 'in bulk', and there is less administration, they can be cheaper than buying privately.

Guaranteed Minimum Pension (GMP)

If your company's final salary pension scheme is contracted-out of the *State Earnings Related Pension Scheme* (SERPS), then it has to guarantee to pay you a certain amount of pension. This is monitored by the Department of Social Security so that your interests are looked after.

Lower Earnings Level

The *Lower Earnings Level* and the Upper Earnings Level are set by the Government each year. *National Insurance contributions* are only paid if an individual earns more than the *Lower Earnings Level*, and individuals don't pay *National Insurance contributions* on earnings above the Upper Earnings Level, but their employers do. Currently (1996/97) the *Lower Earnings Level* is £61 a week and the Upper Earnings Level is £455 a week.

GLOSSARY OF MAIN TERMS

Money purchase
This is a type of pension plan where the size of contributions, rather than the benefits, are defined. The fund managers invest your contributions in an effort to build you up a nice fund by the time you retire. On retirement, you must use this money to buy an *annuity*.

National Insurance contributions
The contributions all employees and the self-employed pay the Department of Social Security help to qualify them for both a pension and other state benefits. How much you pay depends on your earnings, but if you earn less than £61 you don't have to pay anything.

Open market option
If you have been contributing to a *money purchase* pension, you must ultimately use your fund to buy an *annuity*. All pension providers must give you an '*open market option*' to buy that *annuity* from the company of your choice. Not all pension providers offer good *annuity* rates, and it always pays to shop round for the best buy, or to get your independent financial adviser to do it for you.

Permanent health insurance (PHI)
This is a type of insurance that covers you against a long-term sickness or disability that prevents you from working. Most company pension schemes include this cover automatically for the company's employees, The benefits are related to the size of your earnings – not your length of service. If you don't belong to a company pension, you should consider buying this cover personally.

Personal Equity Plans
These are a form of savings plan, based on the unit trust principle, in

which any gains you make are free of either income tax or capital gains tax. They are ideal vehicles for supplementing your pension planning.

Personal pensions

Personal pensions were introduced in July 1988 to encourage self-employed people, or employed people who were not in a company pension scheme, to make their own provision for retirement. They are eminently suitable for the self-employed. All types of *personal pension* are very tax-efficient plans for retirement.

Protected rights

Using a SERPS rebate to contract-out of the *State Earnings Related Pension Scheme* in order to invest the money in your own *personal pension* scheme, has some conditions which may not suit you. For instance, that part of your *personal pension* for which you paid with the SERPS rebate will be 'ring fenced' by the insurance company and you will not be able to draw that part of your *personal pension* until you are 60. Also, you cannot draw a lump sum from that part.

Rebate-only pension

See *Appropriate Personal Pension*

Retirement Annuity Plans

Also known as *Section 226 pension plans*, these are old-style *personal pensions* which were mainly sold to the self-employed. They were overtaken by the more flexible *personal pension* plans, and haven't been available to newcomers since 1988.

Section 32 Buy-out policies

This is an insurance company policy which you can buy with the money built up in a company pension scheme after you have left it. You use it to buy an *annuity* when you retire.

Section 226 pension plans See *Retirement Annuity Plans*

Tax Exempt Special Savings Accounts (TESSAs)
Available mainly from banks and building societies. *Tax Exempt Special Savings Accounts* are specially devised for savers wanting a secure home for their money. To get full advantage of them you need to invest for a full five years, but you can draw off an income if you are prepared to sacrifice the potential for growth. You can invest up to £3,000 in the first year and up to a total of £9,000 over the five years.

INDEX

actuary 193
added years 33, 193
additional pension (1) 193
additional pension (2) 194
additional voluntary contributions (AVCs) 22, 67-73, 194
annual bonus 127
annuities 159, 173-182, 189, 195
appropriate personal pension (APP) 21, 103, 107-109, 195

basic state pension 43-45
bonus 195
buy-out plans 195

carry-back arrangement 26, 196
commute 67, 196
company pensions 21-22, 59-94, 162-163
　opting out of a 87-91, 120
COMPS 196
contracting out 21, 196

death in service benefits 91, 196
deferred annuity 197
deferred pensions 79-81
deposit accounts 186
deposit based plans 130
deposit based schemes 131
die, what will happen if I? 91-94
divorced women 47

early leavers 78-79, 197
early retirement 52-53, 160
earnings cap 63-64, 197
employers contributions 113-114
expression of wish form 92

final salary 61-63
final salary schemes 73-74, 197
financial advisor, how to choose one 142-145
flexible pension 184
freestanding AVCs, FSAVCs 69, 197

graduated pensions 49
group personal pensions 77, 198
Guaranteed Income Bonds 188
Guaranteed Minimum Pension (GMP) 65, 198

hybrid pension schemes 77-78
income PEPs 189

late retirement 53
life cover 120-121
lower earnings level 48, 198
lump sum 118, 170-172, 185, 190

married women's career break 46-47
married women's stamp 45-46
money purchase schemes 22, 74-77, 163-164, 198

National Insurance contributions 198
National Savings Pensioners income Bonds 186-187
open market option 119, 199

paying contributions 97-99
pensions, how much will you need? 16
  how much will you contribute 26-27
  20-somethings 24-29
  30-somethings 29-32
  40-somethings 32-36
  50-somethings 36-39
Pensions Scheme Registry 23
permanent health insurance (PHI) 199
Personal Equity Plans (PEPs) 147-157, 189, 199
personal pensions 95-145, 164-166, 199
pin-money pensions 120
Protected rights 112, 118
purchased life annuities 189

retirement at 50 115-120, 166-172
retirement, annuity plans 200
  at normal age 166-167
  phased 184
retiring late 167-169

salary sacrifice 37
Section 32 Buy-out policies 200
self administered schemes 121-122
self-employed 47-48
SERPS 48-51, 64-65
  contacting out 110-113
  rebate 103-107
  rebate only pension 28
spouses 49
  pension 182-183
state, what it provides 41-58
state pensions 20-21, 41-58, 160-162
  forecast 49-51
  when can you draw? 51-56

tax 148-149
Tax Exempt Special Savings Accounts (TESSAs) 187-188, 200
tax relief on contributions 99-103
top-up options 53-58
transfer values 83-87
types of plan 126-130

unitised with-profits 129
unit-linked 127-129
upper earnings level 48

with profits 126-127
  versus unit-linked 130-141

REFERENCE SOURCES

Annuity Bureau
Enterprise House, 59-65 Upper Ground, London SE1 9PQ

Bacon & Woodrow
St. Olaf's House, London Bridge City, London SE1 2PE

Benefits Agency
For local office, see listing in your local telephone directory

Chase de Vere Investments
63 Lincoln's Inn Fields, London WC2A 3BR

Contributions Agency
Contributions Query Section, Longbenton, Newcastle upon Tyne NE98 1YX

Department of Social Security (DSS)
For local office, see listing in your local telephone directory
DSS Pensions Information Line: 0345 313233
DSS Pensions Freepost BS5555/1, Bristol BS99 1BL

THE COMPLETE GUIDE TO PERSONAL PENSIONS

Independent Financial Advisers Promotion (IFAP)
17-19 Emery Road, Brislington, Bristol BS4 5PF
Helpline: 0117 971 1177

***Money Management* magazine**
49-50 Poland Street, London W1V 4AX

National Association of Pension Funds
12-18 Grosvenor Gardens, London SW1W 0DH

Pensions Scheme Registry
PO Box 1NN, Newcastle upon Tyne NE99 1NN

Personal Investment Authority (PIA)
1 Canada Square, Canary Wharf, London E14 5A2
Central Register: 0171 929 3652

Securities and Investments Board
Cotton Centre, Cottons Lane, London SE1 2QB

***The Private Investor's Guide to the Stockmarket*
by Neil Stapley**
Published by Rushmere Wynne Limited, 4-5 Harmill, Grovebury Road, Leighton Buzzard, Bedfordshire LU7 8FF

Rushmere Wynne

are publishers of finance, investment and management books.
If you would like a copy of our current catalogue

Please write to:
Rushmere Wynne
4-5 Harmill
Grovebury Road
Leighton Buzzard
Bedfordshire
LU7 8FF

or Fax: 01525 852037

or Phone: 01525 853726